POEMS OF THE MASTERS

Poems of the Masters

千
家
詩

China's Classic Anthology of
T'ang and Sung Dynasty Verse

translated by RED PINE

Copper Canyon Press
A Kage-an Book

Cover art: *Scholar,* Anonymous, Sung Dynasty. Courtesy of the National Palace Museum, Taipei, Taiwan, Republic of China.

Copper Canyon Press is in residence under the auspices of the Centrum Foundation at Fort Worden State Park in Port Townsend, Washington. Centrum sponsors artist residencies, education workshops for Washington State students and teachers, Blues, Jazz, and Fiddle Tunes festivals, classical music performances, and the Port Townsend Writers' Conference.

LIBRARY OF CONGRESS CATALOGING-IN-PUBLICATION DATA
Poems of the masters: China's classic anthology of T'ang and Sung dynasty verse / Translated by Red Pine. — 1st ed.
     p.   cm.
English and Chinese.
Includes index.
ISBN 1-55659-195-0
1. Chinese poetry — T'ang dynasty, 618–907 — Translations into English. 2. Chinese poetry — Sung dynasty, 960–1279 — Translations into English. I. Title: China's classic anthology of T'ang and Sung dynasty verse. II. Pine, Red.
PL2658.E3P634 2003
895.1'1308 — DC21

                                                        2003004949

9 8 7 6 5 4

Kage-an Books (from the Japanese, meaning "Shadow Hermitage" and representing the "shadow work" of the translator) presents the world's great poetic traditions, ancient and modern, in vivid translations under the editorship of Sam Hamill.

COPPER CANYON PRESS
Post Office Box 271
Port Townsend, Washington 98368
www.coppercanyonpress.org

for Burton Watson

Contents

PART TWO

PART THREE

PART FOUR

POEMS OF THE MASTERS

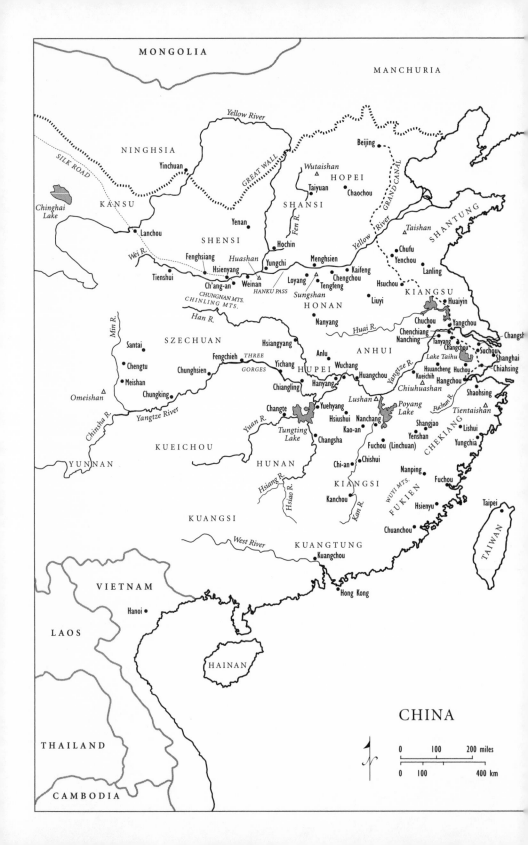

Translator's Preface

Poetry is China's greatest art. No matter how wonderful its painting and calligraphy, its pottery and bronze casting, its sculpture and architecture, its music and dance, or its other literary arts, none of these has ever gained the universal appreciation and participation that poetry has enjoyed. This was especially true of the Middle Kingdom's T'ang (618–906) and Sung (960–1278) dynasties, which Chinese ever since have called their Golden Age of Poetry. During the T'ang and Sung, poetry became the defining measure of human relationships and human understanding. Nothing was significant without a poem: no social or ritual occasion, no political or personal event was considered complete without a few well-chosen words in rhyme that summarized the subtleties of the Chinese vision of reality and that linked this vision with the beat of their hearts. Although this universal art form had been developing in China for millennia, its greatest flowering was in the T'ang and Sung, when suddenly it was everywhere: in the palace, in the street, in every household, every inn, every monastery, in every village square.

I don't pretend to be able to explain the complex social changes that helped bring about this efflorescence in the T'ang and Sung, but by examining the word itself we can at least see why poetry held such an important place in Chinese culture. The Chinese word for poetry is *shih* (詩) and is composed of two parts. The part on the left (言) means "language," and the part on the right (寺) originally meant "administrative court" and later came to mean "Buddhist temple." But this was not the original form of the part on the right, and neither "court" nor "temple" has anything to do with the meaning of *shih*. This is because the second part was originally written *chih* (志), meaning "from the heart," and the later form was simply the result of calligraphic shorthand and subsequent convention. Hence, the word for poetry does not mean the "language of the court/temple" but the "language of the heart." The Great Preface to the *Book of Odes* says, "When it's in the heart, it's *chih*. When it's expressed in language, it's *shih*." Thus, since the dawn of Chinese civilization 5,000 years ago, it has been the function of poetry to express this innermost square-inch of the Chinese heart.

China's earliest known book of this "language of the heart" was the *Shihching*, or *Book of Odes*. This is a collection of ritual hymns, ballads, and folk songs that date back to the beginning of the Chou dynasty around 1100 B.C. Some are even said to have been passed down from the time of Yu the Great, founder of the Hsia dynasty in 2205 B.C. The collection itself is attributed to Confucius (551–479 B.C.), who reportedly sifted through some 3,000 poems from various parts of China and finally selected 305 as suitable for use in instructing his disciples.

Another collection of equal, if not greater, importance was the *Chutzu*, or *Songs of Ch'u*. This was a collection of the poems of Ch'u Yuan (340–278 B.C.) and other shaman-literati of the state of Ch'u compiled by an anonymous editor around the beginning of the Christian Era. Unlike the *Book of Odes*, the *Chutzu* contained the work of known individuals. And unlike the more aloof and stylized *Odes*, the poems in the *Chutzu* poured forth far more personal and heartfelt joys and sorrows. As a result, this book had a much greater impact on poets. Wang Wei (701–761) once said he carried two books with him wherever he traveled: the *Vimalakirti Sutra* and the *Chutzu*.

As time went on, other collections of poetry appeared. But aside from the *Book of Odes* and the *Songs of Ch'u*, no other anthology gained more than a limited audience—until the appearance of the *Chienchiashih*, or *Poems of the Masters*. This collection was first compiled at the end of the Sung dynasty by one of its most prolific writers, Liu K'o-chuang (1187–1269). Liu was also a leading literary critic, and at some point he decided to present his views on poetry through a collection of examples. Although no copy of Liu's original anthology still exists, we know that he chose about 200 poems and arranged his selections under fourteen headings: flowers, bamboo, the sky, the earth, palace life, weather, tools, music, animals, insects, seasons, festivals, daily events, and human character. It was a great success. And as it enjoyed the good fortune of being published at the beginning of China's printing revolution, it soon appeared in village schools and private academies across the country, where it established itself as eminently useful in teaching students the rhythms of language and also the heart, as well as the names of all sorts of things an educated person should know.

Over the centuries, Liu's original edition was rearranged by different editors, and the number of poems increased to the present 224. In some editions, several poems dating from the Ming dynasty (1368–1643) were also added to this total, but I have followed most editors in deleting them as extraneous.

At the beginning of the seventeenth century, Wang Hsiang, who is better known for his works for and about women, rearranged the poems into four parts according to poetic form: 39 four-line poems with five characters to a line, 45 eight-line poems with five characters to a line, 94 four-line poems with seven characters to a line, and 46 eight-line poems with seven characters to a line. Readers interested in Chinese poetics should note that the four-line poems all follow the rhyme schemes and tonal patterns laid down for *chueh-chu* (detached quatrains), and all eight-line poems follow the more complex rules for *lu-shih* (regulated verse) that required a great deal of parallelism as well. Wang also arranged the poems in each section according to the seasons (more or less), and he composed the first commentary. Wang's version of Liu's anthology became so popular that the previous editions disappeared altogether, and I have generally followed Wang's arrangement.

The Chinese title of this book is *Ch'ien-chia-shih*, which literally means *Poems of a Thousand Masters*. There are, however, only a hundred or so poets represented; hence, I have dropped the numeral. Despite the exaggeration, *Poems of the Masters* includes the most-quoted poems in the Chinese language by the most famous poets of China's Golden Age of Poetry. And for the past eight centuries, it has been the most-memorized collection of verse in China and part of every student's education.

When Sun Chu (1711–1778) published *Three Hundred Poems of the T'ang* in 1763 — and *Poems of the Masters* finally had to share the poetry stage — Sun said in his preface that he based his own collection on the earlier anthology, and he admitted it was superior to his in terms of its shorter, easier-to-memorize poems. Although Sun's collection eventually proved more popular with older readers, *Poems of the Masters* retained its preeminent place in the education of every schoolchild, as its emphasis on four-line poems made it much more useful in teaching poetry to students at an earlier age. Although China's recent detour into communism saw the *Chienchiashih* replaced in schools with proletarian propaganda, it was still part of the national curriculum until the middle of the last century. And I suspect it will be again someday. Its success, like that of *Three Hundred Poems of the T'ang*, has been in large part due to its inclusion of poems that could be understood and appreciated by all sectors of society. And its poems are as meaningful today as they were when they were written.

In addition to translating the poems in this collection, I have included the original text for those able to read Chinese. I have also added a certain amount of background information to help readers locate these poems in time and space and in the lives of the poets. Scholars, however, are not always in agreement concerning events of a thousand or more years ago, and my choice among different accounts simply reflects what has seemed to me the most likely. But even without such information, and even if they did not fully understand the context in which these poems were written, the Chinese have always appreciated their "language of the heart" and continue to quote their phrases and lines in their speech today. Hence, I can think of no better way to reveal that hidden square-inch every Chinese holds dear and depends upon for inspiration than through this modest collection of poems.

Red Pine
Cold Dew, Year of the Horse
Port Townsend, Washington

TRANSLATOR'S ACKNOWLEDGMENTS

My thanks for the continuing support of the U.S. Department of Agriculture's Food Stamp Program, the Port Townsend Food Bank, the Olympic Community Action Energy-Assistance Program, the Earned Income Tax Credit Program administered by the Internal Revenue Service, and the American Optometric Association's Vision USA Program.

PART ONE

1

春曉　孟浩然

春眠不覺曉　處處聞啼鳥
夜來風雨聲　花落知多少

Meng Hao-jan (689–740) was one of the foremost poets of the T'ang and one of the few who did not pursue an official career. When Meng was forty, the retired prime minister, Chang Yueh, invited him to the western capital in Ch'ang-an to take the civil service exam. But Meng not only failed, he annoyed Emperor Hsuan-tsung as well, and he soon returned to his family estate outside Hsiangyang. When time permitted, and it usually did, Meng visited friends at their posts along the Yangtze or enjoyed the peace of the hermitage he built on Lumenshan, twenty kilometers southeast of his home. Five centuries earlier, the recluse P'ang Te-kung also built his hut on the same mountain. Like P'ang, Meng had little interest in worldly goals and preferred to sleep late—while his friends in the capital were at court before dawn. Even as winter becomes spring, Meng is still sleeping late and isn't wakened by the sun but by the sound of birds

Spring Dawn

MENG HAO-JAN

Sleeping in spring oblivious of dawn
everywhere I hear birds
after the wind and rain last night
I wonder how many petals fell

beginning their spring courtship. Still, this too fails to drive him from his bed, and he is content to wonder about the scene outside without feeling the need to do anything about it.

2

訪袁拾遺不遇　孟浩然

洛陽訪才子　江嶺作流人
聞說梅花早　何如此地春

Loyang was the T'ang dynasty's eastern capital and was located at the edge of the Yellow River floodplain, 300 kilometers north of Meng's home. Although he remained an outsider, Meng's reputation as a poet made him welcome in the highest levels of society. But on this trip he failed to meet an official to whom he had written earlier. The man had been demoted for taking the responsibilities of his post too literally — censors were charged with reporting improper conduct and harmful policies to the emperor — and he had been banished to Chiangling, the mountainous area of the Tayu Range that separates the Kan River watershed from the semitropical South. Meng sent this poem to express both his disappointment and his sympathy. In the temperate North, the plum flowers during the lunar New Year and marks the start of spring, which is a time when families make every effort to be together.

Calling on Censor Yuan without Success

MENG HAO-JAN

In Loyang I tried to visit you sir
to Chiangling you were banished
the plum I hear flowers earlier there
but how could spring compare

3

送郭司倉　王昌齡

映門淮水綠　留騎主人心
明月隨良掾　春潮夜夜深

Wang Ch'ang-ling (698–756) was from the Ch'ang-an area but spent most of his career in low-level posts in outlying provinces. Not long after the An Lu-shan Rebellion broke out in 755, he resigned his post in Hunan but was murdered on his way back north. He wrote this poem c. 739 while serving in Nanching after a brief banishment to Kuangtung province. The Huai is one of China's major rivers and flows parallel to the Yangtze one hundred kilometers north of Nanching. But Wang is referring to a much smaller river of the same name (usually called the Chinhuai) that emptied into the Yangtze from the south at Nanching. Although Wang did not enjoy success as an official, he was well known for his short poems, especially those on the subject of farewell. Here, he tries to detain a friend whose official duties included supervision of government granaries that supplied farmers with seed and grain at a set price. With the advent of spring planting, his

Seeing Off Supply Director Kuo

WANG CH'ANG-LING

Huai River green brightens my door
this host would keep a traveler longer
the moon leaves too with an honest official
but every night spring waters grow deeper

friend heads west up the Yangtze, followed by the moon, while Wang takes
solace in the thought that the Yangtze will not only continue to link their
hearts together but also will deepen with spring rains.

4

洛陽道　儲光羲

大道直如髮　春日佳氣多
五陵貴公子　雙雙鳴玉珂

Ch'u Kuang-hsi (707–760) was born just west of Chufu in Shantung province and passed the country's highest civil service exam at the unusually young age of nineteen. He rose to become an imperial inspector, but when the armies of An Lu-shan swept through Loyang in 755, he was forced to serve in the rebel administration. After the rebellion was crushed, he was sentenced to death but was sent into exile instead and died soon after reaching his post. This was one of five poems he wrote for his fellow poet Lu Ssu-lang. When Loyang was rebuilt during the Sui and early T'ang, it was laid out west of the old city with straight, wide roadways. During the T'ang, it served as the dynasty's eastern capital, while Ch'ang-an served as the western capital. The Wuling Hills were northwest of Ch'ang-an and named for a group of five imperial grave mounds. This was also where many well-to-do families maintained estates, and the name eventually became associated with the western capital's elite, whether or

The Roads of Loyang

CH'U KUANG-HSI

The roads are as straight as strands of hair
and full of the glories of spring
the noble young lords from the Wuling Hills
ride by in pairs with their bridles ringing

not they had estates at Wuling. Here, the sons of the elite are in the eastern capital, which was famous for its gardens during the T'ang, racing one another on horses whose bridles are decorated with cowry shells from the South Seas.

5

獨坐敬亭山　李白

眾鳥高飛盡　孤雲獨去閒
相看兩不厭　只有敬亭山

Li Pai (701–762) aka Li Po, and Tu Fu are ranked as China's two greatest poets. Li was born in what is now Kyrgyzstan and grew up in Szechuan north of Chengtu. For a brief period he was a favorite of the court, but he soon fell into disfavor and spent most of his life wandering along the Yangtze, a guest of those who appreciated his talent and unrestrained spirit. He wrote this poem in 753, during one of several stays in Hsuancheng, a town south of Nanching still famous for its rice paper. Chingting Mountain was five kilometers northwest of the old city wall. Although its peak was only 300 meters high, it was known for its crags and cliffs and was also where the poet Hsieh T'iao (464–499) wrote many of his most famous landscape poems. On this visit, Li observes the transience of the world around him and his separation from it. But he also becomes aware of his oneness with the mountain. According to a tradition at least as old as Confucius, water represents wisdom (teaching us an awareness of

Sitting Alone on Chingting Mountain

LI PAI

Flocks of birds disappear in the distance
lone clouds wander away
who never tires of my company
only Chingting Mountain

impermanence) and mountains represent compassion (teaching us an awareness of the unchanging nature we share with all things). The images here also extend beyond the natural world: the birds represent officials, the lone clouds represent solitary spiritual seekers, and the mountain is the Tao.

6

登鸛鵲樓　王之渙

白日依山盡　黃河入海流
欲窮千里目　更上一層樓

Wang Chih-huan (688–742) was born in Taiyuan, the provincial capital of Shansi, and later moved to Hsinfeng near the southern end of the same province. When a career in the civil service failed to yield anything but minor appointments, he returned home and spent his time visiting friends and traveling to scenic spots in the area. Wang wrote this poem on a visit to Yungchi, one hundred kilometers south of Hsinfeng. The tower he climbed rose three stories above the southwest corner of the city wall and looked out on the Chungtiao Mountains to the south (which are so high — and the sun's trajectory sufficiently low — the noon sun disappears briefly behind their highest peaks). To the west was the Yellow River, which turned east just after it flowed past Yungchi and headed for the sea one thousand kilometers away. The tower was named for the oriental white storks (*Ciconia boyciana*) that roosted on its roof, and many poets

Climbing White Stork Tower

WANG CHIH-HUAN

> The midday sun slips behind mountains
> the Yellow River turns for the sea
> trying to see for a thousand miles
> I climb one more story

commemorated the view. Although Wang was famous for his short poems, and many became standard fare for female entertainers during his lifetime, only six survive.

7

観永樂公主入蕃　孫逖

邊地鶯花少　年來未覺新
美人天上落　龍塞始應春

Sun T'i (fl. 720) was from Poshan in Shantung province and served in several prominent posts, including the Secretariat. During every dynasty, the Chinese court resorted to marriage as part of its foreign policy to foster peaceful relations with the nomadic tribes along its borders. In order to elevate their status with their prospective husbands, daughters of the nobility were honored with the title of "princess" prior to their departure. This particular "princess" was a daughter of the prominent Yang clan and was married to the king of the Khitans, Li Shih-huo, in the last month of 717. Apparently, another spring was too much for the Khitan chieftain, and he died the following year. Dragon Pass (Lungsai) was on China's northeast border with Manchuria, between what are now Blue Dragon Manchurian Autonomous County (Chinglung Mantsu Tzuchihhsien) and Black Dragon County (Lulunghsien). In the *Chuantangshih* (*Complete Poems of the T'ang*), the full title is "With Li Shao-fu of Loyang Seeing Princess Yung-lo Leave for Manchuria."

On Seeing Princess Yung-lo Leave for Manchuria

SUN T'I

Orioles and flowers on the border are rare
even at New Year nothing looks new
but when a beauty falls from Heaven
Dragon Pass finally sees spring

8

春怨　金昌緒

打起黃鶯兒　莫教枝上啼

啼時驚妾夢　不得到遼西

Chin Ch'ang-hsu (fl. eighth century) was a native of Hangchou but has left no other traces than this solitary poem. In some editions, it is entitled "Yichouko" ("Song of Yichou") and attributed to Ko Chia-yun (T'ang dynasty). While the authorship is a moot point, this alternative title is clearly a mistake, as Yichou was just west of the present oasis of Hami on China's northwest border, while Liaohsi was just inside the Great Wall along China's northeast border with Manchuria. The oriole, like the robin, is a harbinger of spring, and the twittering of mating birds only reminds this wife of her separation from her husband.

Spring Complaint

CHIN CH'ANG-HSU

Chase the orioles away
don't let them sing in the tree
their singing disturbs a wife's dreams
and keeps her from reaching Liaohsi

9

左掖梨花　丘為

冷艷全欺雪　餘香乍入衣
春風且莫定　吹向玉階飛

Ch'iu Wei (694–789) was from Chiahsing in Chekiang province and served in the central government before retiring from his final post as tutor to the crown prince. The Chinese have always admired skin not darkened by the sun or dried by the wind — the signs of manual labor and old age. Although this poem ostensibly refers to the imperial harem, and the imperial pear orchard was near the women's apartments, there were pear trees elsewhere in the Forbidden City. Also the title makes it clear that Ch'iu is using the pear blossom's purity to represent the virtue of such court officials as himself, who seek to be of service to the Son of Heaven despite the transience of such recognition. The "jade" steps of white marble at the entrance of the palace in Ch'ang-an represent the imperial presence, and the East Wing was the location of the Chancellery, where Ch'iu was serving at the time and from which he hoped to rise to the emperor's attention — which he did, but as the result of his filial piety rather than his service at court.

A Pear Blossom in the East Wing

CH'IU WEI

Its pristine beauty could fool the snow
its lingering scent soaks through clothes
tell the spring wind not to stop
blow it toward the steps of jade

思君恩　令狐楚

小苑鶯歌歇　長門蝶舞多

眼看春又去　翠輦不曾過

Ling-hu Ch'u (766–837) was born in the Silk Road oasis of Tunhuang and reached the rank of prime minister under Emperor Hsien-tsung (r. 805–820). As a court official, he was known for his elegant essays and poems, and he was once asked by the emperor to compile an anthology of poetry, which has since been lost. Here, he takes on the persona of a concubine among other concubines (the butterflies) who have fallen out of favor with the emperor (the oriole). During the Han dynasty, Emperor Wu (r. 140–87 B.C.) tired of his empress and had her moved to Towering Gate Palace (Changmingkung), at the rear of the Forbidden City. But she became so distraught she paid the poet Ssu-ma Hsiang-ju one hundred kilos of gold to write an ode on her behalf. The emperor was moved, and he brought her back to the main palace. Ironically, Ling-hu himself once paid a bribe of two million strings of cash for a governorship, but here he offers a poem. In Chinese poetry, birds and butterflies invariably appear

On Thinking of My Lord's Grace

LING-HU CH'U

> The oriole's song is gone from my garden
> butterflies dance by the towering gate
> I've watched another spring pass
> without seeing your kingfisher carriage

together, and the absence of one accentuates the isolation of the other. Yet,
though this woman (or official) no longer enjoys the emperor's attention,
her (or his) sentiments, like those of the Han-dynasty empress, have not
changed. Whenever the emperor visited someone, he arrived in a carriage
festooned with pennants that included the iridescent blue-green feathers
of the kingfisher.

11

題袁氏別業　賀知章
主人不相識　偶坐為林泉
莫謾愁沽酒　囊中自有錢

Ho Chih-chang (659–744) was a native of Shaohsing and a member of a group of poets from Chekiang province who formed a literary coterie in Ch'ang-an. Although he served in a series of prestigious posts, including vice-minister of the Ministry of Rites and director of the Palace Library, he was better known for his clever conversation and love of drinking. Tu Fu included him among the Eight Immortals of Wine, and his friends called him the Wild Man of Ssuming (a mountain range east of his hometown). With his fellow intellectuals, he also shared a love of seclusion. During the T'ang it was quite common to maintain a retreat in the Chungnan Mountains south of Ch'ang-an, and it was also during the T'ang that the expression "Chungnan Shortcut" came into use, whereby many would-be officials tried to gain the notice of the court through their "seclusion." Shortly before he died, Ho became a Taoist priest himself and retired to the countryside near Shaohsing.

On Mister Yuan's Country Retreat

HO CHIH-CHANG

We've never met good sir
I stopped because of the woods and stream
don't worry about buying wine
I have some coins in my purse

12

夜送趙縱　楊炯

趙氏連城璧　由來天下傳

送君還舊府　明月滿前川

Yang Chiung (650–694) was born east of Ch'ang-an at the foot of the sa-
cred peak of Huashan. He was recognized as a prodigy as a youth and
served in the staff of the heir apparent and later in several midlevel ca-
pacities. But in 685, when a distant relation staged a minor revolt, he was
banished to Szechuan. A few years later he was recalled to Empress Wu's
court in Loyang. But in 693 he was banished again, this time to Chekiang,
where he died the following year. This poem may have contributed to his
final banishment, as it implies that the emperor (or empress, in this case)
has broken his (or her) word. This connection comes from an account in
Ssu-ma Ch'ien's *Shihchi* (*Records of the Historian*): The King of Chao once
possessed a rare jade disk for which the state of Ch'in offered to exchange
fifteen cities along their common border. The King of Chao gave the disk
to his chief minister to convey to the King of Ch'in. But after discovering
that the King of Ch'in had no intention of honoring his pledge, the

Seeing Off Chao Tsung at Night

YANG CHIUNG

Scion of Chao jade disk worth cities
long has your name been known
seeing you off on your way home
moonlight fills the waiting river

minister refused to give up the disk and returned it to his own king. Here, Yang compares his friend to the jade disk, while its celestial counterpart lights the scene of their parting on the banks of the Yellow River just north of Loyang. His friend is on his way home to Chaochou, the ancient capital of the state of Chao, whose name his friend shares. Yang was considered one of the greatest poets of the early T'ang, though only thirty or so poems survive.

深林人不知　明月來相照
獨坐幽篁裏　彈琴復長嘯

竹里館　王維

Wang Wei (701–761) was from Taiyuan, the capital of Shansi province, and moved to Ch'ang-an as a young man. After passing the civil service exam he rose through the ranks and, despite the occasional banishment, eventually reached the post of vice prime minister. However, his interest in Buddhism blunted any political ambitions, and whenever he had time he preferred to wander in the Chungnan Mountains south of the capital. Wang was not only one of the greatest poets of the T'ang, he was also a skilled musician and one of the dynasty's greatest landscape artists. This was one of twenty poems he wrote toward the end of his life at his Wang (a different Wang) River estate, which was located in a hidden valley some sixty kilometers southeast of Ch'ang-an. Bamboo Retreat was the name he gave to one of several structures he built there. The first line is from Ch'u Yuan's "Shankuei" ("Mountain Spirit"): "Sitting alone amid dense bamboo / I can't see the sky"; and which ends, "the wind whistles / trees sigh

Bamboo Retreat

WANG WEI

Sitting alone amid dense bamboo
strumming my lute and whistling
deep in the forest no one else knows
until the bright moon looks down

/ thinking of you / how useless such grief." The last line of Wang Wei's
poem also recalls the first of three poems titled "Drinking Alone beneath
the Moon," written by Li Pai the night before he left the capital for good
in 744. The Chinese are fond of saying the same moon shines on those
who are apart, thus joining them together.

14

送朱大入秦　孟浩然

遊人五陵去　寶劍值千金
分手脫相贈　平生一片心

Meng Hao-jan (689–740) wrote this poem for a friend who was leaving to seek his fortune (and, no doubt, an official post) in the capital of Ch'ang-an, which was situated in the middle of what was once the ancient state of Ch'in and which retained that state's name. Wuling was the name of a group of imperial grave mounds northwest of Ch'ang-an. As royalty and the rich maintained estates there, the name came to stand for the capital's elite as well as for the capital itself. No member of the gentry would consider himself properly attired at court without a sword, but the sword Meng gives his friend is of a different sort and more valuable, because it can cut through duplicity. In the background here are references to Wu Tzu-hsu (fifth century B.C.), who gave his sword to a fisherman for saving his life and said, "This sword is engraved with the seven stars of the Big Dipper and worth a ton of gold" (*Yulan*: 74), and to Chi Cha, who left on a mission and stopped to see his friend Hsu Chun. Chi was aware that Hsu

Seeing Off Chu Ta Leaving for Ch'in

MENG HAO-JAN

For an unemployed gentleman bound for Wuling
a first-rate sword is worth a ton of gold
I remove this in parting and give it to you
a simple piece of my heart

secretly admired his sword, but he needed it for his mission. When he re-
turned and learned that Hsu had died, he removed his sword and hung it
on a tree beside Hsu's grave. (*Shihchi*)

15

長干行　崔顥

君家何處住　妾住在橫塘
停船暫借問　或恐是同鄉

Ts'ui Hao (704–754) was from Kaifeng and established his reputation as a poet in Ch'ang-an while still in his teens. During this early period his verse followed the carefully regulated usages of court poetics, but he soon broke free into nonconformist technique as well as unrestrained behavior. He was greatly admired by Li Pai. And like Li, he annoyed as many people as he impressed and did not enjoy a successful career. Hengtang (Cross Dike) was the embankment along the Chinhuai River, from Nanching's southwest gate to the Yangtze ten kilometers to the west; the area where the two rivers met was called Changkan (Longpole). Here, the poet speaks through a young girl who is a member of the boat people who still make up separate cultural and linguistic groups in South China. This was the first of four poems. In the second, Ts'ui presents the boy's answer: "My home overlooks the Great River / I travel along the Great River's banks /

Ballad of Changkan

TS'UI HAO

Where are you from good sir
this maid is from Hengtang
I ask while our boats are moored
perhaps we're from the same place

I'm from Longpole too / but I've never seen you before." Longpole ballads, characterized by exchanges between a boy and girl from Changkan, were also written by other T'ang poets.

16

詠史 高適

尚有綈袍贈
應憐范叔寒
不知天下士
猶作布衣看

Kao Shih (702–765) grew up in Honan province in a family sufficiently impoverished that he had to beg for food. But through tenacity he gained an education and eventually an appointment as a secretary in the military. He was one of the few great poets of the T'ang who enjoyed a successful career. Here, he refers to the biography of Fan Shu (aka Fan Sui) in the *Shihchi*. Fan accompanied Hsu Chia as an aide on a mission from Wei to the state of Ch'i, whose king ignored Hsu but presented Fan with delicacies and gold. Hsu suspected Fan had divulged state secrets, and when they returned to Wei he reported this to the prime minister, who had Fan beaten and left for dead. Fan, however, managed to escape, changed his name, and rose to the rank of prime minister in the state of Ch'in. When Fan heard that the state of Wei was sending Hsu on a mission to Ch'in, he disguised himself as a pauper and met Hsu at his inn. When Hsu saw his former aide in such straits, he took off his silk robe and gave it to the man

Ode to the Past

KAO SHIH

He made a gift of his robe
concerned Fan Shu was cold
but unaware of his noble rank
he still saw a common man

he had once maligned. Fan then revealed his new identity, and Hsu ex-
pected to be executed. But Fan pardoned Hsu because of his compassion
for an old friend. Kao, however, condemns Hsu for his blindness and
offers this oblique critique of those in power who fail to discern the true
qualities of others.

17

罷相作
李適之

避賢初罷相
樂聖且銜杯

為問門前客
今朝幾個來

Li Shih-chih (d. 747) was a royal clansman and rose to the rank of vice prime minister. At court he was known for his poetry and love of wine, and he was ranked alongside Li Pai and Ho Chih-chang in his passion for both. As early as the third century, the Chinese referred to unfiltered rice wine as the *hsien* (able) and filtered rice wine as the *sheng* (sage). Thus, the poet's seemingly polite remark in the first line implies he has been replaced by someone less worthy, while he consoles himself in the knowledge of his own virtue. Despite his apparent status and prestige, Li Shih-chih ended up on the wrong side of the infamous prime minister, Li Lin-fu, and was forced to resign in 746. The following year he was sent to a provincial post and ordered to commit suicide. This poem was written following his "resignation" and prior to his departure. During this brief period, he served as a counselor to the heir apparent. But those who once sought out his hospitality are now avoiding him, lest they be associated with a man whose days are numbered.

Resigning as Minister

LI SHIH-CHIH

Yielding my post to the able
enjoying the sage in a cup
I asked someone who came in the past
how many will visit today

18

逢俠者　錢起

燕趙悲歌士　相逢劇孟家
寸心言不盡　前路日將斜

Ch'ien Ch'i (722–780) was from Chekiang province and enjoyed a modest career as an official in both Ch'ang-an and Loyang. Though he never served in anything but minor posts, he was highly regarded as a poet. A generation younger than Wang Wei, he was considered Wang's poetic successor by many, and he was the best known of the Ten Talents of the Tali Period (766–779). Although several hundred poems survive, they have suffered the neglect of later critics, and Ch'ien is not well known today. Yen and Chao were ancient states of North China. In the preface to "Seeing Off Tung Shao-nan," Han Yu (768–824) notes that both states were known for their troubadours. Here, the man to whom Ch'ien writes this poem takes on the persona of the troubadour, with its tragic overtones. Chi Meng lived in Loyang during the Han dynasty and was famous for his chivalrous deeds. In the third line, the feelings that cannot be expressed are perhaps best not expressed. The final line suggests this man is being banished to

On Meeting a Chivalrous Man

CH'IEN CH'I

Singer of elegies of Yen and Chao
we meet where Chi Meng lived
words can't exhaust this inch of our hearts
the sun is setting on the road ahead

some distant post, perhaps on the Silk Road (where the sun sets), as punishment for his "chivalry." Perhaps he was involved in the An Lu-shan Rebellion (755–762) or made the mistake of praising some aspect of it. The states of Yen and Chao were An Lu-shan's base, and Loyang was the capital of his short-lived Greater Yen dynasty.

19

江行望匡廬　錢珝

咫尺愁風雨　匡廬不可登

祇疑雲霧窟　猶有六朝僧

Ch'ien Hsu (fl. tenth century) was a great-grandson of Ch'ien Ch'i, to whom this poem is incorrectly attributed in some editions. Hsu began a promising career in the capital after passing the civil service exam in 898, but he was soon implicated in a political scandal and was sent to serve as the prefect of Nanchang, the capital of Kiangsi province, just south of Lushan. During the Six Dynasties (222–589), Lushan became known for the recluses who made it their home during what was one of the longest periods of instability in Chinese history. The mountain was first named Kuanglushan after one such recluse, K'uang Heng, who moved there during the reign of Emperor Ch'eng (r. 32–7 B.C.). In fact, *k'uang-lu* means "K'uang's hut." Later, K'uang's name was dropped, and it was simply called Lushan, or Hut Mountain. Ch'ien had hoped to climb its slopes on his way to his new post. But Lushan is famous for its mist, and Ch'ien had to content himself with viewing its half-shrouded peaks from his boat and

Traveling on the Yangtze

CH'IEN HSU

So close but plagued by wind and rain
I can't climb Kuanglushan
I wonder if in those mist-hidden caves
any Six Dynasty monks still dwell

wondering if any sages had survived the last period of disunion. As this poem was written, the T'ang dynasty (618–906) was coming to end. This was sixty-ninth in a series of one hundred poems Ch'ien wrote while on this journey.

20

答李澣　韋應物

林中觀易罷　溪上對鷗閒
楚俗饒詞客　何人最往還

Wei Ying-wu (737–792) was born in Ch'ang-an into a well-connected fam-
ily and was allowed to serve in a number of minor posts without having
to pass the civil service exam. After the usual ups and downs, he ended his
career as the prefect of a series of towns along the lower reaches of the
Yangtze, where he wrote this poem. Wei's poetry is often compared to that
of the country poet T'ao Yuan-ming (365–427), who lived in the middle
reaches of the Yangtze in what was once the state of Ch'u, and who was the
model for many who yearned for a life of simplicity. But Ch'u was also
the home of the great shaman-poet Ch'u Yuan (340–278 B.C.), who chose
moral purity over adapting to the ever-changing Tao. As his friend returns
to his post in Ch'u, Wei wonders which of these paths his friend will take.
In the first two lines, Wei answers his friend's question concerning the
direction of his own life. Wei says he has stopped reading the *Yiching*
(*Book of Changes*) and cultivating a life of solitude. Now, instead of trying

In Reply to Li Huan

WEI YING-WU

> I left the *Yiching* in the woods
> now I drift with the gulls by the stream
> among the singers of the ways of Ch'u
> to whom do you most often turn

to predict change, he simply accepts whatever comes, like the gulls. According to a story in *Liehtzu*: 2.11, gulls only relax around those who don't harbor thoughts of catching them. This was the third of three poems.

21

秋風引

劉禹錫

何處秋風至　蕭蕭送雁群

朝來入庭樹　孤客最先聞

Liu Yu-hsi (772–842) was born in the Grand Canal town of Hsuchou to a family of Confucian scholars. Although he held several important posts, such as advisor to the heir apparent and vice-minister in the Ministry of Rites, he was twice demoted because of poems he wrote satirizing those in power. The autumn wind reminds Liu of the end of the summer of his life and of the loss of imperial favor. Like the geese, he is headed south, away from the capital from which he has been banished. But unlike the geese, he is traveling alone. The courtyard is that of a travelers' inn.

Ode to the Autumn Wind

LIU YU-HSI

Where does the autumn wind come from
rising it sees off the geese
entering courtyard trees at dawn
it wakes a lone traveler first

22

秋夜寄丘員外　韋應物

懷君屬秋夜　散步詠涼天
山空松子落　幽人應未眠

Wei Ying-wu (737–792) wrote this poem to Ch'iu Tan, the younger brother of Ch'iu Wei. Wei Ying-wu was serving as prefect of Suchou at the time, and Ch'iu Tan had served briefly as his secretary. However, Ch'iu decided he would rather cultivate the Tao, and he quit his post, crossed the Yangtze, and retired to a hermitage on Pingshan, just outside the northwest gate of Yangchou. Pingshan was also the location of Taming Temple. Several decades earlier, the Buddhist monk Chien-chen left this temple and traveled to Japan, where he is credited with introducing Buddhism, Chinese medicine, and the Chinese language to the Japanese. Thus, the slopes of Pingshan, which was not a large mountain, were not exactly deserted. Still, this was the eighth full moon, or the Mid-Autumn Festival, when relatives and friends normally spend the night together, and Wei tries to imagine how lonely his friend must feel. Pine nuts remain an important source of food for recluses in China. But here, Wei uses them to

To Secretary Ch'iu on an Autumn Night

WEI YING-WU

Out walking and singing of cooler days
I think of you on an autumn night
pinecones falling on deserted slopes
the recluse I suspect not yet asleep

emphasize Ch'iu Tan's isolation, where the only sound is that of falling pinecones. Note, too, that the summers are sweltering in this part of China, and any sign of autumn is welcome—especially the first breath of cool air.

23

秋日　耿湋

返照入閭巷
憂來誰共語
古道無人行
秋風動禾黍

Keng Wei (fl. 770) was a native of Yungchi in Shansi province and served for many years as an imperial advisor. At the peak of his career he was ranked among the court poets known as the Ten Talents of the Tali Period (766–779), among whom he was the least ornate. Although little is known about his later years, this poem suggests he fell out of favor and was forced into simpler lodgings, where he is struck by the strong but fading light that returns to his lane after its journey across the southern sky (for differences of opinion over the meaning of *fan-chao* [returning light], see Eliot Weinberger's *Nineteen Ways of Looking at Wang Wei*). In the background is "Swaying Millet" from the *Shihching* (*Book of Odes*), which describes the area southwest of Ch'ang-an, where the Chou-dynasty capital of Hao once stood, and where Keng is now apparently living. Its author paces the roadway, as if looking for something, and repeats the refrain: "Those who know me / know cares fill my heart / those who don't / wonder

Autumn Day

KENG WEI

The day's late light fills a village lane
with whom can I share my cares
nobody takes the ancient road
millet sways in autumn wind

what I have lost." Hao was destroyed by nomads as the result of the in-attention of King Yu (r. 781–771 B.C.). Keng is concerned that the lessons of history may not have been learned by those now in power—the year is late. Thus, the "ancient road" refers to the Tao as well as to the road leading to a capital that no longer exists.

24

秋日湖上　薛瑩

落日五湖遊　煙波處處愁
浮沉千古事　誰與問東流

Hsueh Ying (fl. 850) has left no information about himself other than what can be gathered from a few surviving poems. The lake on which he is sailing is Taihu (Great Lake), which was also called Wuhu (Five Lakes) because it was said to be made up of five bodies of water, like the petals of a plum blossom. It is one of the largest freshwater lakes in China and is located just south of the Yangtze, not far from where the river meets the sea. The Chinese began migrating to this region at the beginning of the first millennium B.C., and the area around the lake soon became the country's major rice- and silk-producing area. It also became the scene of some of China's most protracted wars. When this poem was written, the region around the lake was so heavily taxed, it was the source of several rebellions, and eventually the court had no choice but to recognize the area's bandit commanders as *de facto* officials. Due to the uplifting of the Tibetan

Autumn Day on the Lake

HSUEH YING

Sailing on the Great Lake at sunset
mist and waves and everywhere sorrow
rising and falling events of the past
who can tell me why they flow east

Plateau, rivers in China generally flow east, and this has become a standard metaphor for the inexorable passage of time. Here, Hsueh wonders why sorrow is its inevitable consequence.

宮中題　李昂

輦路生秋草　上林花滿枝
憑高何限意　無復侍臣知

Li Ang (809–840) was the name of Emperor Wen-tsung (r. 827–840). Following his failed attempt to resolve the bitter factional strife at court in the autumn of 835, the eunuchs made him a virtual prisoner in the palace, and he died of a chronic illness a few years later. He was, however, a man who loved simplicity and enjoyed poetry and wine in equal measures. Here, he looks out from the balcony above the palace wall in the spring of 836 and considers his plight. Even though he is the emperor, he has lost the prerogatives of his position and cannot even visit the royal orchard, which covered thousands of acres west of the palace and which was famous for its pear blossoms. The weed-covered path reminds the emperor that he has not been able to leave the palace since his attempt to assassinate the eunuchs failed the preceding fall. As the only males besides the emperor in the inner palace, eunuchs often wielded more power than government ministers during the reigns of weak emperors—or weak ministers. Implicit

Written in the Palace

LI ANG

The Shanglin Woods are in bloom
but autumn weeds hide the royal path
my ministers no longer know
how vast is the view from on high

here is the emperor's sense that only the Son of Heaven understands the
duty of caring for the realm, which even his confinement cannot dimin-
ish, while the eunuchs, and those officials who carry out their will, are
only concerned with their own welfare.

26

尋隱者不遇　賈島

松下問童子　言師採藥去
只在此山中　雲深不知處

Chia Tao (779–843) was born near Beijing and became a Buddhist monk in his youth. He later changed his mind and decided to return to lay life so that he could devote himself to poetry. He spent all but his final years in Ch'ang-an living in impoverished, if refined, circumstances among those who shared his love. The mountain he visits here is in the Chungnan Range south of Ch'ang-an, where tens of thousands of recluses have lived over the past three millennia. It is still customary for eminent monks and nuns to be accompanied by a young attendant, even when they retire — as many still do — to the cloud-shrouded slopes that rise beyond China's cities and towns. Such recluses collected herbs not only for their own use in elixirs and medicinal decoctions but also to exchange for necessities such as salt and cooking oil, lamp oil, flour (in North China) or rice (in South China), and the occasional new blanket or robe.

Looking for a Recluse without Success

CHIA TAO

Below the pines I ask the boy
he says his master has gone to find herbs
he's somewhere on this mountain
but the clouds are too thick to know where

27

汾上驚秋　蘇頲

北風吹白雲　萬里渡河汾
心緒逢搖落　秋聲不可聞

Su T'ing (670–727) grew up just west of Ch'ang-an and was greatly admired for his prose as well as his poetry. His father, Su Kuei, served as prime minister during the reigns of Chung-tsung (r. 705–710) and Juitsung (710–712), and Su T'ing held the same post during the early years of Hsuan-tsung's reign (712–756). In 720, however, he fell out of favor and was demoted to military governor of Szechuan. He eventually returned to the capital in 724 and was able to live his final years in relative peace. But before he was allowed to do so, he was sent to inspect frontier defenses along the Great Wall in the northern part of Shansi province, which is drained by the Fen River. After coming down from Mongolia, autumn clouds move south across the river while Su, after an equally long journey from Szechuan, crosses it on his way north. The first two lines paraphrase a famous poem by Emperor Wu (r. 140–87 B.C.) of the Han dynasty entitled "Autumn Wind": "Autumn wind stirs and white clouds fly... aboard

Surprised by Autumn on the Fen

SU T'ING

The North Wind blows white clouds
a thousand miles and across the Fen
the hopes of my heart shudder and fall
the sounds of autumn are hard to bear

a rocking boat I cross the Fen." In the last two lines Su is not only surprised by autumn but also by the first signs of his own old age — not decrepitude (he is only fifty-four), but the end of his political career and his imminent forced retirement at the end of this, his last mission.

28

蜀道後期　張說

客心爭日月　來往預期程

秋風不相待　先至洛陽城

Chang Yueh (667–731) was a native of Loyang and was considered by many to be the greatest poet of the early eighth century. He was also an advisor of several emperors who held him in the highest regard. Upon Chang's death, Emperor Hsuan-tsung (r. 712–756) declared two days of national mourning. Chang, however, also suffered numerous rustications to outlying provinces. He wrote this poem after he returned home from "assignment" to Szechuan, via the road that led north from Chengtu to Ch'ang-an and then east to Loyang. Following an earlier banishment to Hunan, Chang's contemporaries noted the change in his poetry from external description to more meditative, introspective verse. Before Chang left Chengtu, he agreed to meet a friend traveling by a different route on the Mid-Autumn Festival in Loyang. Chang arrived home later than expected. But is it the lateness of his arrival that surprises him, or his own old age, or the death of someone dear to him?

Delayed on the Szechuan Road

CHANG YUEH

A traveler races the sun and moon
coming and going according to plan
but autumn wind doesn't wait
it reaches Loyang before me

29

靜夜思　李白

床前明月光　疑是地上霜
舉頭望明月　低頭思故鄉

Li Pai (701–762), aka Li Po, was born in what is now Kyrgyzstan and grew up in Szechuan, north of Chengtu. Ranked with Tu Fu as one of China's two greatest poets, he left behind over one thousand poems. This is one of his most famous, and critics sigh at the effortlessness of his technique and his ability to transport the reader not only to a place but also to a state of mind. When the Chinese see the moon, it reminds them that friends and family members living elsewhere are looking at the same moon.

Thoughts on a Quiet Night

LI PAI

Before my bed the light is so bright
it looks like a layer of frost
lifting my head I gaze at the moon
lying back down I think of home

30

秋浦歌　李白

白髮三千丈
緣愁似箇長
不知明鏡裏
何處得秋霜

This was number fifteen in a series of seventeen poems Li Pai wrote in 754, while visiting the town of Kueichih in Anhui province. Kueichih still serves as a minor port for Yangtze River traffic, but it is better known nowadays as the gateway for pilgrims visiting the Buddhist mountain of Chiuhuashan. In Li Pai's day, Chiuhuashan (Nine Flower Mountain) was just another mountain — its name comes from one of his poems — and he preferred to wander along the Chiupu River southwest of town. This poem is often cited as an example of Li Pai's romantic style. But our version of reality is forever at the mercy of our emotions, and this is about as realistic a poem as Li Pai could have written at this stage of his life. When he later died downriver from Kueichih, the story that circulated was that he drowned while trying to embrace the moon and that, while his body was buried nearby, his spirit flew up to Heaven on the back of a whale. Or maybe it wasn't a whale: between Kueichih and the place where he

Chiupu River Song

LI PAI

My white hair extends three miles
the sorrow of parting made it this long
looking in a mirror who would guess
where autumn frost comes from

reportedly drowned is a nature sanctuary for the sightless Yangtze dol-
phin. Chinese mirrors were made of convex palm-sized pieces of polished
metal that were held in the hand and covered up when not in use.

31

贈喬侍郎　陳子昂

漢庭榮巧宦　雲閣薄邊功
可憐驄馬使　白首為誰雄

Ch'en Tzu-ang (661–702) was a native of Szechuan province and served in a series of midlevel posts, including that of censor. He was regarded as one of the most innovative poets of the early T'ang and was also admired for his concern with social issues, a concern that led to his death at the hands of his political enemies. Here he offers his sympathy to a friend, Ch'iao Chih-chih, whose talents (and, no doubt, Ch'en's own) he feels could be put to better use. Both men at one time served together on the Silk Road. Instead of criticizing the court directly, Ch'en aims his remarks at the Han court of eight hundred years earlier for allowing civil servants and syco-phants to oversee military affairs along the border—while those truly capable of such service wasted their talents standing in attendance in the capital. During the Han, the walls of the palace's Cloud Pavilion (the com-bined structures of Cloud Terrace and Unicorn Pavilion) were covered with paintings of those who performed meritorious service but excluded

To Vice Censor Ch'iao

CH'EN TZU-ANG

The Han court glorified clever officials
Cloud Pavilion disdained border service
pity the master of dapple-gray steeds
what good is an old man's valor

exemplars of military and civil valor, such as generals and censors. The
title, "master of dapple-gray steeds" (*tsung-ma-shih*), Ch'en bestows on his
friend (and on himself), was originally an epithet of the Han-dynasty
censor Huan Tien, whose carriage was pulled by a team of gray horses.

32

答武陵太守　王昌齡

仗劍行千里　微軀敢一言
曾為大梁客　不負信陵恩

Wang Ch'ang-ling (698–756) was from the Ch'ang-an area but spent most of his career out of favor and in low-level posts in outlying provinces. Here, he stops in Wuling on his way back from banishment to Kueichou province. This Wuling was not the Wuling Hills of Ch'ang-an but the area west of Tungting Lake whose administrative center was located in the city of Changte on the Yuan River. This was the first Chinese city of any size Wang would have encountered after leaving the frontier outpost of Liping near the headwaters of the Yuan, 700 kilometers to the southwest. Thus, he expresses his relief in having survived the dangers of the road as well as his appreciation for not having been forgotten. In ancient times, the Lord of Hsinling, Wei Wu-chi, was known for housing and caring for over 3,000 guests at a time at his estate in Taliang (Kaifeng), the capital of the state of Wei. While Wang's comparison might seem an exaggeration, it should be

In Reply to the Prefect of Wuling

WANG CH'ANG-LING

Still clutching my sword after a long journey
this servant dares but a word
a guest of the Lord of Hsinling
never forgets such kindness

remembered that he is returning from a year of monitoring hilltribes in a
region that must have seemed inhospitable, if not outright dangerous, to
a Chinese intellectual.

33

行軍九日思長安故園　岑參

強欲登高去　無人送酒來

遙憐故園菊　應傍戰場開

Ts'en Shen (715–770) was born in Nanyang and grew up in Loyang, but once he began his official career he maintained an estate at the foot of the Chungnan Mountains south of Ch'ang-an. In addition to several provincial assignments, he twice served on the Silk Road. Following the fall of Ch'ang-an to the rebel army of An Lu-shan in 755, forces loyal to the throne first retreated to Yinchuan and then returned as far as Fenghsiang in 756. Ts'en joined them en route from his post on the Silk Road. T'ang forces retook the capital the following fall. Chrysanthemums bloom in fall, and a wine infused with their petals is traditionally drunk on the ninth day of the ninth moon. As nine is the perfect *yang* number, this is the ultimate *yang* holiday, when men celebrate their virility and congratulate one another on having lived so long. In the first line, Ts'en refers to the Chinese custom of climbing a hill or tower from which to enjoy the view on this holiday, a custom traced back to Huan Ching of the Han

Thinking of My Home in Ch'ang-an While Traveling with the Army on the Ninth

TS'EN SHEN

If only I could climb somewhere
but no one sends me wine
my poor distant garden of mums
blooms by a battlefield now

dynasty (206 B.C.–A.D. 220). In the second line, he recalls an occasion when T'ao Yuan-ming (365–427) found himself without wine on Double Ninth and sat disconsolate in his garden until the local prefect heard of his plight and sent him a jug.

34

婕妤怨　皇甫冉

花枝出建章　鳳管發昭陽
借問承恩者　雙蛾幾許長

Huang-fu Jan (716–769) was born in Kansu province but grew up near Nanching and was known for his poetry and prose even as a boy. Although he served in a number of posts, he never achieved the success he expected and here wonders why. The woman whose persona he appropriates was Pan Chieh-yu, the great aunt of the historian Pan Ku (A.D. 32–92) and a concubine of Emperor Ch'eng of the Han dynasty (r. 32–7 B.C.). Although the emperor admired her virtue and learning, he later became infatuated with Chao Fei-yen and sent Pan to live by herself in Changhsing Palace. There, she wrote poems complaining of neglect, and later writers often used her voice to point to their own overlooked abilities. In ancient China, eyebrows were considered one of a woman's greatest assets, much like breasts are today in the West. Thus, Pan compares hers to those of the other women at court. During the Han dynasty, Chienchang

A Concubine's Lament

HUANG-FU JAN

A flowering branch grows from Chienchang Palace
from Chaoyang Hall I hear the royal flutes
I wish I could ask those favored few
exactly how long are their eyebrows

Palace was built by Emperor Wu and was said to have one thousand doors
and ten thousand windows. Emperor Ch'eng built Chaoyang Hall directly
behind it as a residence for Chao Fei-yen.

35

題竹林寺　朱放

歲月人間促　煙霞此地多
殷勤竹林寺　更得幾回過

Chu Fang (fl. 750–790) was from Hsiangyang in Hupei province. After a brief career in the civil service, he retired to a hermitage on the Shan River in Chekiang province and lived there as a recluse. Some years later, he accepted a sinecure as an advisor to the military commissioner of Kiangsi and moved to the provincial capital in Nanchang. Here he visits Lushan, two days' journey to the north. Chulin (Bamboo Grove) Temple was also called Holin (Crane Forest) Temple and was among the most famous sights on Lushan's mist-shrouded slopes. The temple was located along the mountain's rocky northwest ridge but has long since disappeared. Although Chu is clearly aware of the temple's separation from his life of civilized ease, he appears to have lost his ability to free himself, as he did earlier, from such mundane existence, and we can only guess why.

Written at Chulin Temple

CHU FANG

The months and years compel our lives
here the mist and clouds abound
how many times will I again know
the welcome of Chulin Temple

36

三閭大夫廟　戴叔倫

沅湘流不盡　屈子怨何深

日暮秋風起　蕭蕭楓樹林

Tai Shu-lun (732–789) was a native of Chintan in Kiangsu province and served for many years as a private secretary in Hunan province. At one point, he was appointed prefect of Nanchang, but during his later years he turned his back on a worldly career and became a Taoist priest. The Yuan and Hsiang are the largest tributaries of Tungting Lake, which itself is often regarded as the final section of the Hsiang before it empties into the Yangtze. It was here that Ch'u Yuan (340–278 B.C.) was exiled for advice that would have saved his ruler, and it was here that he drowned himself rather than live in an unjust world. The Three Gates (San Lu) refer to Ch'u Yuan's inherited position as overseer of the three royal lineages, and also to his ancestral fief near Tzukuei in the middle of the Yangtze's Three Gorges. Some commentators place this shrine in Milo, not far from the place where Ch'u Yuan drowned himself in a tributary of the Hsiang. Others say it was on the Yuan River near the modern town of Huaihua,

Passing the Shrine to the Master of the Three Gates

TAI SHU-LUN

The waters of the Yuan and Hsiang never cease
Ch'u Yuan's grief is so deep
the autumn wind rises at sunset
and blows through a grove of maples

where Tai was serving as a private secretary at the time. The last two lines
rise from the final lines of Ch'u Yuan's "Chaohun" ("Summoning the
Soul"), where the red maple leaves represent the blood of his heart.

37

易水送別　駱賓王

此地別燕丹　壯士髮衝冠

昔時人已沒　今日水猶寒

Lo Pin-wang (640–684) was born in Chekiang, grew up in Shantung, and was ranked as one of the four great poets of the early T'ang. When he was a young man he became a Taoist priest. But later he decided to seek a position in Ch'ang-an, where he was in and out of favor. At one point he was banished to the Silk Road oasis of Turfan, and on another to a distant outpost in Southwest China. Finally, for opposing Empress Wu's usurpation, he was jailed and banished to the Chekiang coast. Not long afterward he joined the rebel Hsu Ching-yeh in Yangchou. But when Hsu's forces were defeated, Lo was among those killed in reprisal—although some say he became a Buddhist monk. Here, he recalls the parting of Prince Yen Tan and Chin K'o, whom Yen was sending to assassinate the tyrant who would soon become China's First Emperor (r. 221–210 B.C.). As the two said goodbye outside the capital of Yen on the banks of the Yi River, not far southwest of modern Beijing, Chin K'o clasped his sword and sang: "The

Saying Goodbye on the Yi River

LO PIN-WANG

> Here where Yen Tan said goodbye
> a hero raised his hat with his courage
> the men of the past are gone
> but the water is still cold today

wind blows hard and the Yi is cold / once a hero leaves he never returns."
Chin K'o was so emotionally aroused, his hair stood on end and lifted his
hat from his head. Despite such resolve, he was killed before he could
complete his mission. As Lo recalls this scene he fears that he too will die
before he is able to rid the country of another tyrant, namely Empress Wu.
But he takes solace in the survival of a courageous man's name.

38

別盧秦卿　司空曙

知有前期在　難分此夜中
無將故人酒　不及石尤風

Ssu-k'ung Shu (740–790) was from Yungnien in Hopei province and served as director of the Bureau of Waterways and Irrigation, and later of the Bureau of Forestry and Crafts. He was ranked among the Ten Talents of the Tali Period (766–779) and was known for the playfulness of his poems, which he wrote on topics such as noodle soup. For such men, spending time together discussing and writing poetry was a major part of their lives. Hence, Ssu-k'ung tries to detain a friend with wine that he compares to a great wind. This wind was named after a woman and her merchant husband. When the husband failed to return from a journey, his wife died of a broken heart. But on her deathbed she vowed, "After I die, my spirit will become a great wind that will prevent all men going on distant journeys from leaving their wives." Thereafter, her name and that of her husband were combined to describe such a departure-preventing wind.

Saying Goodbye to Lu Ch'in-ch'ing

SSU-K'UNG SHU

I know we plan to meet again
but how can we part tonight
don't think an old friend's wine
is weaker than a Shihyu Wind

39

答人 太上隱者

偶來松樹下 高枕石頭眠
山中無曆日 寒盡不知年

Nothing is known of the author of this poem, other than that he lived in the Chungnan Mountains south of Ch'ang-an and called himself T'ai-shang ying-che (The Ancient Recluse). Here, he replies to someone who has asked him why and how long he had been living there. He dismisses the first question with *ou-lai* (somehow/by chance) and the second question with *wu-li-jih* (no calendar) and then laughs at the idea of time-constrained concerns. The phrase *kao-mien* (sleeping in comfort) comes from the precept that prohibits Buddhist monks and nuns from using excessive bedding. Its use here is meant to emphasize the poet's detachment from the usual standards of comfort as well as from precepts. The last line also recalls the story of the refugees who escaped to the hidden world of Peach Blossom Spring and, upon being discovered, wondered what dynasty it was.

In Reply

Somehow I ended up beneath pines
sleeping in comfort on boulders
there aren't any calendars in the mountains
winter ends but who counts the years

PART TWO

40

幸蜀回至劍門　玄宗皇帝

劍閣橫雲峻　鑾輿出狩回
翠屏千仞合　丹嶂五丁開
灌木縈旗轉　仙雲拂馬來
乘時方在德　嗟爾勒銘才

Hsuan-tsung (685–762) was one of China's greatest emperors (r. 712–756) but was also greatly flawed, as he took little interest in government affairs and devoted himself instead to the arts, religion, and his concubine Yang Kuei-fei. After one of the longest reigns in China's long history, he fled to Western Szechuan (the ancient state of Shu) in the summer of 756, as the rebel armies of An Lu-shan approached Ch'ang-an from the east. His son, meanwhile, established a temporary capital in Ninghsia province, north-west of Ch'ang-an, and had himself enthroned as Emperor Su-tsung. When the An Lu-shan Rebellion was more or less crushed the following autumn, the new emperor invited his father back, and here Hsuan-tsung euphemistically refers to his absence as having been "on tour." He also refers to the five legendary strongmen who were traveling through these mountains when they saw a huge snake disappear into a cave and tried to pull it out by its tail. Their efforts caused a landslide that crushed them

Reaching Sword Gate Pass After Touring the Land of Shu

HSUAN-TSUNG

> Our tour complete our carriage returns
> to Sword Gate's cloud-barred peaks
> its mile-high screen of folded jade
> its cinnabar walls breached by heroes
> our pennants weave through a tapestry of trees
> ethereal clouds brush past our horses
> rising to the times depends upon virtue
> how true is this inscription

to death but also resulted in the opening of a more accessible route. As the former emperor reached Sword Gate Pass (Chienmenkuan — 250 kilometers northeast of Chengtu) in the winter of 757, he turned to his attendants and said, "Although the natural barrier of Sword Gate is immense, has its ability to prevent communication since ancient times not depended on its virtue rather than its height?" His comment and the poem he wrote on this occasion were inspired by an inscription left at the pass in A.D. 281 by Chang Tsai. Chang recalled an earlier conversation between Duke Wu of the state of Wei (fl. fourth century B.C.) and Wu Ch'i, in which the duke called mountains and rivers the treasures of the state, and Wu replied that their virtue and not their strategic significance was their true value (*Shih-chi*: 44). Thus, it would seem that Hsuan-tsung finally realizes that his neglect of state affairs has led to his own undoing.

41

和晉陵陸丞相　杜審言

獨有宦遊人　偏驚物候新
雲霞出海曙　梅柳渡江春
淑氣催黃鳥　晴光轉綠蘋
忽聞歌古調　歸思欲沾巾

Tu Shen-yen (646–708) was a native of Hsiangyang in Hupei province and moved with his father to Kunghsien, east of Loyang, which was where his grandson, Tu Fu, was born. He held important posts in the court of Empress Wu Tse-t'ien (r. 684–705) but was better known for his poetry and calligraphy and is considered one of the founders of T'ang-style verse. Following Empress Wu's death he fell out of favor, and in 705 he was exiled to what is now North Vietnam. He was soon recalled and given a sinecure in the capital, but the experience had a major effect on the poetry of his final years. Here, apparently during his banishment to the South, he responds to a poem by his friend Lu Yuan-fang, who had served as prime minister during the reign of Empress Wu and who had retired to his home in Chinling (Changchou) on the Grand Canal. Lu's poem (now lost) noted how much earlier spring appeared south of the Yangtze than in the capital. Tu begins by referring to himself as a *huan-yu* (impotent official),

Replying to a Poem by Prime Minister Lu of Chinling

TU SHEN-YEN

Only an impotent official
is truly surprised when things become new
red clouds giving birth to the ocean dawn
plums and willows ferrying spring across the river
clear skies inciting yellow birds
sunshine turning duckweed green
suddenly hearing a familiar tune
I think of home and dry my eyes

which was a term officials often used out of humility but also when they were sent off to the provinces. By itself, *huan* refers to a palace eunuch. Tu's use of the term underlines his political status and loss of faith in the world's power of renewal, as well as the government's inability to break free of the chains of tradition. Thus, he is surprised by spring. The orioles remind him of his wife back in the capital, but the rootless duckweed reminds him of his life on the road. And the familiar tune is the poem to which he replies.

42

蓬萊三殿侍宴奉敕詠終南山　杜審言

北斗掛城邊　南山倚殿前

雲標金闕迥　樹杪玉堂懸

半嶺通佳氣　中峰繞瑞煙

小臣持獻壽　長此戴堯天

In this poem, Tu Shen-yen is attending the emperor's birthday celebration at one of the three main halls of Taming Palace in Ch'ang-an. This hall was named for the island of immortals that still appears off the coast of Shantung from time to time and to which Taoist adepts hope to be transported after shedding this mortal form. The mountains to which Tu compares the emperor are the Chungnan Mountains, which rose thirty kilometers south of Ch'ang-an, and which were also called the Nanshan, or Southern Mountains. Their name was a metaphor for immortality, and Tu uses them here to transport the emperor's earthly realm to the celestial plane. A poem in the *Shihching* (*Book of Odes*) goes: "The smile of the moon / the glory of the sun / the age of Nanshan / by change untouched." The Northern Dipper is a symbol not only of old age but also of leadership, as all the stars revolve around it. And the golden gates and jade halls are characteristic of the celestial realm but are also used as euphemisms for the

At an Imperial Banquet in Penglai Hall Offering Praise for the Chungnan Mountains

TU SHEN-YEN

The Northern Dipper hangs beside the wall
the Southern Mountains lean before the palace
golden gates appear in distant clouds
jade halls float above the trees
a noble air spreads across the slopes
a propitious mist circles the central peak
your servant offers wishes for long life
long may you keep the ways of Yao alive

imperial residence. Yao was a legendary emperor who ruled China during the third millennium B.C. Confucius once sighed, "Great was Yao's rule! How magnificent he was! It is only the Celestial Realm that is great, and only Yao who modeled himself on it" (*Analects*: 8:19). Yao's ancestral fief was the kingdom of T'ang, and his reign was called the "Reign of T'ang." Hence, this last reference suggests this poem was written following Tu's return from exile in 706. In that year the capital also returned from Lo-yang to Ch'ang-an. But after the interregnum of Empress Wu, it was still uncertain if the re-establishment of the T'ang dynasty and re-enthronement of Emperor Chung-tsung (r. 705–710) would last. Thus, while offering birthday congratulations, Tu also reminds the emperor of his ancestral responsibility to uphold the Mandate of Heaven for the benefit of all those under his care.

43

春夜別友人　陳子昂

銀燭吐清煙　金樽對綺筵
離堂思琴瑟　別路繞山川
明月隱高樹　長河沒曉天
悠悠洛陽道　此會在何年

Ch'en Tzu-ang (661–702) was from Szechuan province and wrote this poem in 688 as he prepared to leave Chengtu for Loyang. As the candles smolder after a night of goodbyes, Ch'en and his friend hear "High Mountains" and "Flowing Waters" in each other's hearts, just as the wood gatherer, Chung Tzu-ch'i, once did in the zither playing of Yu Po-ya. And as they toast each other they recall the Weaving Maid and Herdboy stars, who were banished by the Sun King to either side of the Milky Way (River of Stars) and are only allowed to meet one night a year. Ch'en fears a longer separation. Following his arrival in Loyang he enjoyed a promising career, but he also made enemies during Empress Wu's usurpation of power. When he finally returned to Chengtu to mourn his father, he was killed by the local prefect at the direction of Wu San-ssu, the empress's nephew.

Parting from a Friend on a Night in Spring

CH'EN TZU-ANG

As black smoke coils from silver candles
we raise gold cups across silk mats
our thoughts are like zithers in this hall of parting
following a path over mountains and streams
the bright moon sinks below tall trees
the River of Stars vanishes at dawn
the road to Loyang leads so far away
what year will it lead back again

長寧公主東莊侍宴　李嶠

別業臨青甸　鳴鑾降紫霄
長筵鵷鷺集　仙管鳳凰調
樹接南山近　煙含北渚遙
承恩咸已醉　戀賞未還鑣

Li Chiao (644–713) served as prime minister during three reigns but was cashiered for his arrogance when Hsuan-tsung ascended the throne in 712. Although his poems on everyday objects were highly esteemed, those written at imperial request, such as this one, were rather superficial and probably included by the editor as examples of the genre. Here, Li records a visit by Chung-tsung (r. 705–710) to his daughter's estate east of Ch'ang-an. Blue is the color of the east, and purple of the royal realm. Mandarins and egrets represent higher and lower officials, and the phoenixes are the princess and her husband. The Chungnan Mountains are to the south, and the Wei River is to the north.

Attending a Banquet at Princess Ch'ang-ning's Eastern Estate

LI CHIAO

Her country estate overlooks a blue domain
carriages come ringing out of a purple sky
mandarins and egrets flock to an endless feast
phoenixes play celestial flute serenades
tree-covered mountains rise to the south
mist-shrouded marshes stretch to the north
everyone is drunk from drinking in such favor
their philanthropic majesties postpone their departure

45

恩賜麗正殿書院宴應制得林字　張說

東壁圖書府　西園翰墨林
誦詩聞國政　講易見天心
位竊和羹重　恩叨醉醴深
載歌春興曲　情竭為知音

Chang Yueh (667–731) was a native of Loyang and rose to the rank of prime minister during the reign of Hsuan-tsung (r. 712–756). In 725, the emperor built a new library to house state documents and also put Chang in charge of writing a dynastic history. At the banquet to honor the occasion, the emperor asked Chang to compose a poem using the word *lin* (forest) to begin the rhyme. The library was in the East Wing, and the Hanlin Academy of scholars was in the West Garden. The *Book of Odes* and *Book of Changes* were the two most studied and quoted Confucian classics. The last line's use of the expression *chih-yin* (to know another's tune or voice) refers to the emperor but originated with the wood gatherer Chung Tzu-ch'i, who was the only person who could understand what was in Yu Po-ya's heart whenever Po-ya played the zither (see also the note to verse 43).

Given the Word "Forest" by His Majesty at the Licheng Palace Library Banquet

CHANG YUEH

In the East Wing's halls of maps and texts
in the West Garden's forest of brushes and ink
we chant the *Odes* and hear the royal directives
we discuss the *Changes* and observe the moods of Heaven
our posts though humble our roles are vital
well favored and supplied with wine
we compose songs on the coming of spring
exhaust our hearts for the one who knows them

46

送友人　李白

青山橫北郭　白水遶東城
此地一為別　孤篷萬里征
浮雲遊子意　落日故人情
揮手自茲去　蕭蕭班馬鳴

Li Pai (701–762) enjoyed a brief period of fame at court but was expelled in 744 and spent the rest of his life wandering, mostly along the Yangtze, looking for patrons and hoping to be recalled to the capital. He wrote this poem in 754 while saying goodbye to a friend in Hsuancheng. Chinese cities were usually protected by two sets of walls: an inner wall of brick or stone and an outer rampart of rammed earth. Between them was enough farmland to supply the town with food during a siege. It was customary for friends to say goodbye at the outer rampart, and there were usually inns capable of supplying farewell fare for every budget. The Shuiyang River still circles what remains of the city's east wall.

Seeing Off a Friend

LI PAI

Dark hills stretch beyond the north rampart
clear water circles the city's east wall
from this place where farewell begins
a tumbleweed leaves on a thousand-mile journey
drifting clouds in a traveler's thoughts
the setting sun in an old friend's heart
as we wave and say goodbye
our parting horses neigh

47

送友人入蜀　李白

見說蠶叢路　崎嶇不易行
山從人面起　雲傍馬頭生
芳樹籠秦棧　春流遶蜀城
升沈應已定　不必問君平

Li Pai was quite familiar with this road, as it ended near his hometown of Chinglien Village, north of Chengtu in Western Szechuan. Western Szechuan was the ancient state of Shu, and it was also called Tsantsung, after Ts'an Ts'ung, a descendent of the Yellow Emperor, who moved there in the third millennium B.C. and established the hegemony of the Han Chinese. The Tsangtsung Road was built in the third century B.C. by the state of Ch'in, in order to invade Shu. The Chinling Mountains that separated the two states were so rugged that the road often gave way to planks supported by thick pegs driven into the rock cliffs. The "walls of Shu" refer to those of Chengtu, and the "currents of spring" to those of the Min River that formed the city's moat. Yen Tsun was a famous Taoist fortune-teller who lived in Chengtu in the first century B.C. In the second half of this poem, Li tries to console his friend by suggesting he look for the silver

Seeing Off a Friend Leaving for Shu

LI PAI

You've heard of the Tsantsung Road
how rugged it is and hard to travel
mountains rise before your face
and clouds appear beside your horse
but the planks of Ch'in are shrouded by fragrant trees
and the walls of Shu are circled by the currents of spring
ups and downs are surely fixed
you don't need to ask Yen Tsun

lining in his rustication and accept his fate, however unjust; even Cheng-
tu's greatest fortune-teller couldn't fathom the whims of those responsible
for his friend's banishment.

48

次北固山下　王灣

客路青山外　行舟綠水前
湖平兩岸闊　風正一帆懸
海日生殘夜　江春入舊年
鄉書何處達　歸雁洛陽邊

Wang Wan (c. 690–740) was from Loyang and never held high office but was well known for his poetry even as a youth. Here, he stops for the night at a small peninsula that juts into the lower reaches of the Yangtze, where the Grand Canal intersects the river and where boats often moored before continuing north or south on the canal, east and out to sea, or west and up the Yangtze. Wang's home was 800 kilometers to the north, and spring arrives much earlier here, reminding him how far away he is. During the Han dynasty, an emperor once shot a goose and found, tied to its foot, a letter written by an official being held against his will by the Huns. Wild geese have been used ever since as the mail carriers of the hopelessly separated. The fifth and sixth lines became so famous that Chang Yueh (667–731) wrote them on the wall of his office as examples of inspired verse.

Stopping at Peiku Mountain

WANG WAN

My route goes past blue peaks
where riverboats ply green water
the current is smooth the shores are wide
the wind is perfect for hoisting a sail
the ocean sun rises in the traces of night
the river spring starts inside the old year
how shall I send a letter home
tied to a goose bound for Loyang

49

蘇氏別業　祖詠

別業居幽處　到來生隱心
南山當戶牖　灃水映園林
竹覆經冬雪　庭昏未夕陰
寥寥人境外　閒坐聽春禽

Tsu Yung (699–746) was born in Loyang and passed the civil service exam in 725. Through the good offices of such friends as Wang Wei, he was able to serve in several minor posts in Ch'ang-an and here visits a friend's retreat southwest of the capital on the Feng River. The second line was not an idle thought. Not long after he wrote this, Tsu resigned his post and retired to a hermitage on the Jushui River, south of his family home in Loyang. The presence of mountains and water are important in choosing a residence, and bamboos represent the indomitable will of a person of humble virtue. However, some editions have *wu-fu* (roofs are covered) in place of *chu-fu* (bamboos bend). The darkened courtyard suggests proximity to mountains as well as the absence of worldly affairs.

Mister Su's Country Retreat

TSU YUNG

Your country retreat is such a quiet place
I think of retiring each time I come
the Chungnan Mountains fill your doors and windows
the Feng River brightens your trees and garden
your bamboos bend with winter-long snow
your courtyard is dark before dusk
beyond the sound and reach of man
I sit and listen to the birds of spring

50

明朝有封事　數問夜如何
不寢聽金鑰　因風想玉珂
星臨萬戶動　月傍九霄多
花隱掖垣暮　啾啾棲鳥過

春宿左省　杜甫

Tu Fu (712–770) wrote this poem in 758 when he was serving as a censor in Ch'ang-an. This position required him to spend the night at the Chancellery next to the palace ("the height of Heaven") and to attend the pre-dawn audience with the emperor. Thus, he is one of the flowers, while the lesser officials, who can go home for the night, are the birds. The palace was said to have one thousand doors and ten thousand windows. The "jade" bridles of the royalty were decorated with cowry shells that looked and sounded like jade (see verse 3). The An Lu-shan Rebellion was not yet over, and Tu Fu wonders about the possible bearing of the sounds he hears in the imperial night. Not long after he wrote this, he was demoted and began a period of wandering that did not end until he died.

Staying Overnight at the Chancellery in Spring

TU FU

Flowers by the palace retire at dusk
nestbound birds call as they pass
stars appear and a thousand doors open
the moon shines brighter near the height of Heaven
the sound of gold locks keeps me awake
were those jade bridles I heard in the wind
morning court brings more sealed dispatches
and questions about last night

51

題玄武禪師屋壁　杜甫

何年顧虎頭　滿壁畫滄州
赤日石林氣　青天江海流
錫飛常近鶴　杯渡不驚鷗
似得廬山路　真隨惠遠遊

Tu Fu saw this mural in 759 at a Buddhist temple near Santai, on his way to Chengtu. Ku K'ai-chih (345–406) was known for his temple art, but Tu Fu simply uses his name to praise the actual artist, who includes scenes of the Taoist island paradise of Tsangchou as well as a few Buddhist monks. Emperor Wu (r. 502–549) once told a Buddhist and a Taoist that whichever of them could place an object first on Chienshan could use the mountain for his hermitage. The Taoist sent his cranes, and the Buddhist sent his magic staff. The mural also depicts the story of a monk who arrived from India in the fifth century in nothing more than a wooden tub. Lieh-tzu once noted that gulls are only frightened by those who think of catching them (2.11). The monk Hui-yuan (334–416) lived on Lushan and began Pure Land practice in China by vowing to be reborn in Amida Buddha's Paradise.

Painted on the Wall of Master Hsuan-wu's Room

TU FU

What year did Tigerhead Ku
cover this wall with scenes of Tsangchou
the red sun and forest of rocks
the blue sky and ocean of waves
a staff forever flying next to a crane
a seaborne tub beside unfrightened gulls
this is like finding the road to Lushan
following the actual steps of Hui-yuan

52

終南山　王維

太乙近天都　連山到海隅
白雲迴望合　青靄入看無
分野中峰變　陰晴眾壑殊
欲投何處宿　隔水問樵夫

Wang Wei (701–761) served in a number of prominent posts in Ch'ang-an, including that of deputy prime minister. His political ambition, however, was never equal to his love for mountains, and he spent as much time at his retreat in the Chungnan Mountains as he did at court. *Taiyi* (The Great One) was another name for the Tao. It was also another name for the Chungnan Mountains and its highest peak. The Heart of Heaven refers to the Taoist paradise as well as to the Son of Heaven's residence. White clouds also represent a life of detachment, and blue vapors worldly aspiration. The Chinese at one time laid out the empire into twenty-eight realms, corresponding to the constellations of the Chinese Zodiac, all radiating from these mountains. Upon meeting a woodcutter, an herb gatherer, or a hermit in the mountains of China, even a stranger soon feels at home.

The Chungnan Mountains

WANG WEI

Taiyi isn't far from the Heart of Heaven
its ridges extend to the edge of the sea
white clouds form before your eyes
blue vapors vanish in plain sight
around its peaks the whole realm turns
in every valley the light looks different
in need of a place to spend the night
I yell to a woodcutter across the stream

53

寄左省杜拾遺　岑參

聯步趨丹陛　分曹限紫薇
曉隨天仗入　暮惹御香歸
白髮悲花落　青雲羨鳥飛
聖朝無闕事　自覺諫書稀

Ts'en Shen (715–770) wrote this poem in 758, one year after returning to Ch'ang-an in Emperor Su-tsung's (r. 756–762) retinue, as the An Lu-shan Rebellion was winding down. He describes the morning assembly at court, where he and Tu Fu were serving at the time. Ts'en was rectifier-of-omissions in the Secretariat and was in charge of criticizing imperial documents and the emperor's own conduct, while Tu Fu was a censor in the Chancellery and was in charge of criticizing officials. The Secretariat was located in the west wing of the courtyard just outside the imperial palace, and the Chancellery was in the east wing. Both were separated by rows of purple myrtle. Not long after he wrote this poem, Ts'en Shen (the rising official) and Tu Fu (the old man) were dismissed from their posts.

To Censor Tu at the Chancellery

TS'EN SHEN

We hurry in pairs up cinnabar steps
our ranks divided by purple myrtle
at dawn we follow the guards inside
at dusk we return trailing perfume
an old man grieves to see petals fall
a rising official envies wild birds
the court of a sage contains no omissions
the work of a censor I imagine is rare

54

登總持閣　岑參

高閣逼諸天　登臨近日邊
晴開萬井樹　愁看五陵煙
檻外低秦嶺　窗中小渭川
早知清淨理　常願奉金仙

Ts'en Shen visited this Buddhist pagoda soon after returning to Ch'ang-an with Emperor Su-tsung's army in 757. The pagoda was on Nanwutai Peak, among the northernmost ridges of the Chinling Range (the Chungnan Mountains). Ch'ang-an was twenty-five kilometers to the north and the Wei River thirty-five. The Chinese count nine heavens. The smoke came from fires set to the estates in the Wuling Hills northwest of the capital by the departing rebel armies of An Lu-shan. Ts'en had spent his life in the entourage of the powerful and now sees their insignificance and relative value and wonders if it would not have been better to possess nothing at all, to live the pure life of a monk rather than that of an official. The "golden immortal" refers to the Buddha.

On Climbing Tsungchih Pagoda

TS'EN SHEN

I climbed a pagoda that touched the highest heaven
I stood at the edge of the sun
I could see ten thousand courtyards below
and the dismal smoke of Wuling
beyond the railing the Chinling looked low
the Wei seemed small in the window
if I had known such detachment before
I would have served the golden immortal

55

登兗州城樓　杜甫

東郡趨庭日　南樓縱目初
浮雲連海岱　平野入青徐
孤嶂秦碑在　荒城魯殿餘
從來多古意　臨眺獨躊躇

Tu Fu (712–770) wrote this poem in 737 after failing the civil service exam and going to visit his father, who was serving as military commander of Yenchou, or East District, where the Yellow River floodplain meets the Shantung peninsula. Looking out from the city's South Tower, Tu Fu is reminded of the inexorable nature of time. Taishan, resting place of spirits, was to the northeast, and the Pohai Sea, home of immortal isles, lay beyond. The rich farmland of Hsuchou and Chingchou was to the east, but it had been impoverished by an imperial tour in 725. Similar results followed a visit in 219 B.C. by the Ch'in dynasty's First Emperor, who left a record of his visit on a stele outside nearby Chufu. Chufu was the capital of the ancient state of Lu and the site of Lingkuang Palace, built in the Han dynasty by Lu Kung. Tu Fu's father was in ill health and died the following year.

Climbing Yenchou Tower

TU FU

Visiting my father in East District
I finally looked out from South Tower
clouds stretched beyond Taishan to the sea
barren land spread through Hsu and Chingchou
the outline of the stele of Ch'in was still there
the walls of Lu Palace were rubble
I've always been drawn to the past
but this time my heart trembled

56

送杜少府之任蜀州　王勃
城闕輔三秦　風煙望五津
與君離別意　同是宦遊人
海內存知己　天涯若比鄰
無為在歧路　兒女共沾巾

Wang Po (647–676) was a child prodigy and later was hailed as one of the four literary lights of the early T'ang. However, he was convicted of murdering a servant and sentenced to death, and his father was banished to Hanoi. Wang was subsequently pardoned, but on his way to join his father he drowned. Here, he parts from a friend heading west from Ch'ang-an and implies that he, too, is leaving for the provinces. Ch'ang-an was in the middle of three administrative districts carved out of the ancient state of Ch'in. Shuchou, his friend's destination, was across the Min River from Chengtu in Western Szechuan (the ancient state of Shu) and was reached by taking one of the five fords along the river.

On Deputy Prefect Tu Taking Up a Post in Shuchou

WANG PO

From walls that guard the realms of Ch'in
through windblown mist to the fords of Shu
we gaze and consider our separation
both of us nomad officials
but still true friends this side of the sea
neighbors on either shore of the sky
where the road forks let us not join
our children drying their tears

57

送崔融　　杜審言

君王行出將　書記遠從征
祖帳連河闕　軍麾動洛城
旌旗朝朔氣　笳吹夜邊聲
坐覺煙塵掃　秋風古北平

Tu Shen-yen (646–708) wrote this poem while serving in Loyang at the court of Empress Wu. As court poet, he was required to attend such grand occasions as the departure of the army. Here, he consoles his friend Ts'ui Jung (653–706), who had been assigned as court secretary to Wu San-ssu, the empress's devious nephew, who was leading an army to the northern frontier. This was a post usually filled by men of promise, but Tu's friend still needs encouraging, which Tu supplies by reminding him that he will be watching and not participating in the fighting. This poem was written in the summer of 696, shortly after the nomadic Khitans invaded Hopei province. T'ang forces were crushed during their initial encounters with the enemy and were not successful in repulsing the invasion until the following summer. Kupei was the name of a strategic pass along the Great Wall, one hundred kilometers northeast of Beijing.

Seeing Off Ts'ui Jung

TU SHEN-YEN

Our sovereign sends forth her general
her secretary joins the distant campaign
farewell tents line palace gates
columns of soldiers shake city walls
with flags and pennants to mark the dawns
and flutes and drums to fill border nights
smoke and dust will rise while you watch
the autumn wind quell Kupei

58

扈從登封途中作　宋之問

帳殿鬱崔嵬　仙遊實壯哉
曉雲連幕捲　夜火雜星回
谷暗千旗出　山鳴萬乘來
扈遊良可賦　終乏掞天才

Sung Chih-wen (d. 712) was from Shansi province and served in important posts in Ch'ang-an and later in Loyang during the reign of Empress Wu. Along with Shen Ch'uan-ch'i (verse 185), he was considered one of the greatest poets of the period following the early T'ang. But when the empress died in 705 the coups and countercoups that followed left him in a vulnerable position. When Jui-tsung re-ascended the throne in 710 (his earlier reign [684–690] ended when Empress Wu established her own reign [690–705]), Sung was exiled to the South and forced to commit suicide. Here, he accompanies Empress Wu at the end of 696 on her way back from performing a sacrificial ceremony at Sungshan—a ceremony normally reserved for emperors at the beginning of a new dynasty and normally performed at the eastern sacred peak of Taishan. Sungshan's summit was the central member of China's five sacred peaks. In ancient times, ten

The Imperial Entourage on the Road from Tengfeng

SUNG CHIH-WEN

A palace of brocade adorns the great peak
the ascent of an immortal is glorious indeed
at dawn curtains weave through the clouds
at dusk lanterns flicker among the stars
countless banners wind out of a dark ravine
down the quaking mountain ten thousand chariots roll
the royal entourage is worthy of an ode
alas I lack the skill to dazzle Heaven

thousand chariots were said to constitute the power of a king. Tengfeng,
seventy kilometers southeast of Loyang, was the county seat at the moun-
tain's base.

59

題義公禪房　孟浩然

義公習禪寂　結宇依空林
戶外一峰秀　階前眾壑深
夕陽連雨足　空翠落庭陰
看取蓮花淨　方知不染心

Meng Hao-jan (689–740) visits a monk friend in his mountain hermitage. The lotus (*Nelumbium*) blooms in early summer and was first cultivated in Egypt, from whence it spread to Assyria and India. It arrived in China, along with Buddhism, via the Silk Road, and has been used ever since as a symbol for transcending the world while remaining rooted in its mud.

Written on the Wall of Master Yi's Meditation Hut

MENG HAO-JAN

Accustomed my friend to the stillness of Zen
you built a refuge in deserted woods
outside the gate a lone peak soars
beyond the steps wind countless ravines
sunset follows a daylong rain
tall trees cover your yard with shade
now that I've seen the lotus in bloom
I know the mind impervious to stain

60

醉後贈張旭　高適

世上漫相識　此翁殊不然
興來書自聖　醉後語尤顛
白髮老閒事　青雲在目前
床頭一壺酒　能更幾回眠

Chang Hsu (fl. 750) was one of China's greatest calligraphers and was famous for his cursive script, which became more inspired as he drank. When I was first living in Taiwan, whenever I had to go to Hong Kong to renew my visa I asked my calligraphy teacher (Chuang Yen, curator of the Palace Museum's Calligraphy and Painting Collection) if I could bring him back brushes or ink, as people in Taiwan were still forbidden to travel to China. But all he ever asked for was Tachu White Lightning. He said he did his best work before dawn, after a cup or two. Chang also loved to drink and was ranked among the Eight Immortals of Wine. It's said he kept a jug beside his bed so he could drink as soon as he woke up. Blue clouds represent high position and refer to his new post as court calligrapher, which required earlier hours than he was used to. Kao Shih (716–765) uses two of Chang's nicknames here: *ts'ao-sheng* (god of shorthand) and *tien* (crazy).

To Chang Hsu after Drinking

KAO SHIH

The world is full of fickle people
you old friend aren't one
inspired you write like a god
drunk you're crazier still
enjoying white hair and idle days
blue clouds now rise before you
how many times will you still sleep
with a jug of wine by your bed

61

浩刼因王造　平臺訪古遊
綵雲蕭史駐　文字魯恭留
宮闕通群帝　乾坤到十洲
人傳有笙鶴　時過北山頭

玉臺觀　杜甫

Tu Fu (712–770) wrote this poem in 763 while attending the funeral of a fellow official in Langchung, 200 kilometers northeast of Chengtu on the Chialing River. This Taoist temple, on Jade Terrace Mountain north of town, was built by King T'eng, the son of Emperor Kao-tsu (r. 618–626), in 679, while the son was serving as prefect of Langchung. Hsiao Shih was a flute player of the sixth century B.C. who became an immortal on Huashan. The inscriptions ostensibly record the construction of Lingkuang Palace by Lu Kung, the son of Emperor Ching (r. 156–141 B.C.), in Confucius's hometown. Taoist immortals reach the islands of the blessed on the backs of cranes. Wang Tzu-ch'iao, the son of King Ling (r. 571–545 B.C.), was often seen riding in this manner playing his flute.

Jade Terrace Temple

TU FU

The palatial steps were built by a king
the terrace resembles those of the past
colored clouds welcome Hsiao Shih
inscriptions record the words of Lu Kung
the shrine halls lead to the realm of the gods
the whole place recalls an immortal isle
people report hearing flutes and cranes
often passing the peak to the north

62

觀李固請司馬弟山水圖　杜甫

方丈渾連水　天臺總映雲
人間長見畫　老去恨空聞
范蠡舟偏小　王喬鶴不群
此生隨萬物　何處出塵氛

Tu Fu wrote this poem in 764 in Chengtu for his friend Li Ku. It was one of three he wrote on this landscape painted by his cousin, who also contributed the funds for Tu Fu's cottage in Chengtu. Fangchang was one of the islands where immortals lived, and the Tientai Mountains were near the Chekiang coast. The Taoist alchemist, Ko Hung (283–343), said that they were the perfect place to cultivate the Tao. Fan Li was a minister of the Warring States Period (433–221 B.C.) who escaped power and fame to spend his days as a recluse near Lake Taihu. And Wang Tzu-ch'iao (aka Wang Ch'iao), son of the Chou dynasty's King Ling (r. 571–545 B.C.), became an immortal and flew off on a crane. Tu Fu wishes Fan's boat could hold another, or that Wang had a second crane. The dust is that of his fellow officials, who crowd the road ahead, but also refers to what Buddhists call "the 'red dust' of sensation."

On Seeing a Landscape Painted by My Commissioner Cousin for Li Ku

TU FU

Fangchang surrounded by water
Tientai all dazzling clouds
I often see their pictures on walls
but I hate such tales in old age
Fan Li's boat is too small
and Wang Ch'iao's crane flies alone
I followed everyone else this life
where can I go to escape the dust

63

旅夜書懷　杜甫

細草微風岸　危檣獨夜舟
星垂平野闊　月湧大江流
名豈文章著　官因老病休
飄飄何所似　天地一沙鷗

Tu Fu wrote this poem in the summer of 765. The death of his patron and protector, Yen Wu, prompted his departure from Chengtu in May. Looking for another place to settle with his family, he headed east. Here, traveling on one of the tall-masted boats that carried passengers on the Yangtze, he wishes he had achieved fame for something other than writing—poets earned no royalties—and for something more worthy of his talents. When he quit his last post he was only forty-six. But age and illness are standard reasons given to avoid criticizing the court for its lack of appreciation. Since the moon is rising after the stars are out, it must be waning—an apt metaphor for Tu Fu's career. Seagulls are rarely alone.

Recording My Thoughts While Traveling at Night

TU FU

A shore of thin reeds in light wind
a tall boat alone at night
stars hang over the barren land
the moon rises out of the Yangtze
how could writing ever lead to fame
I quit my post due to illness and age
drifting along what am I like
a solitary gull between Heaven and Earth

64

登岳陽樓　杜甫

昔聞洞庭水　今上岳陽樓
吳楚東南坼　乾坤日月浮
親朋無一字　老病有孤舟
戎馬關山北　憑軒涕泗流

Tu Fu wrote this poem at the end of 768, after sailing through the Yangtze Gorges. He had hoped to continue north to his home near Loyang, but invading Turk armies made such a journey too dangerous. As far back as Ch'u Yuan (340–278 B.C.), Tungting Lake was synonymous with exile, and the area was a common assignment for those out of favor. Yuehyang Tower was at the northeast corner of the lake—not far from where it merges with the Yangtze—and also where the ancient kingdoms of Wu and Ch'u met. The tower was first built during the Three Kingdoms Period (A.D. 221–265) as an observation platform for naval maneuvers and was rebuilt several times. This version was built in 716 by Chang Yueh during his exile to Yuehyang. Tu Fu lived on this boat with his family until his death a year or so later. He was buried ninety kilometers southeast of Yuehyang.

Climbing Yuehyang Tower

TU FU

I heard long ago about Tungting Lake
here I am climbing Yuehyang Tower
where Wu and Ch'u divide South from East
where Heaven and Earth and day and night drift
of family and friends I have no news
old and sick I live on a boat
warhorses block the northern passes
my tears fall on the railing

65

楚山不可極　歸路但蕭條
海色晴看雨　江聲夜聽潮
劍留南斗近　書寄北風遙
為報空潭橘　無媒寄洛橋

江南旅情　祖詠

Tsu Yung (699–746) was born in Loyang and served briefly in the government, but he retired at an early age to a hermitage south of Loyang. Here, he finds himself at the end of winter on an unwelcome mission to Changsha, the capital of Hunan. The Mountains of Ch'u extend from southern Hunan to northern Kiangsi and are named for the ancient state that once ruled this region. The sword represents Tsu's accoutrement of office, while his letters, flying the opposite direction of migrating geese (which are themselves the mail carriers of the hopelessly separated), convey the interests of his heart. The Southern Dipper is only visible south of the Yangtze. Changsha was known for the oranges that grew on an island in the Hsiang River. They were a welcome present at New Year, as their color represented abundance and happiness.

Traveling South of the Yangtze

TSU YUNG

The Mountains of Ch'u never end
the only road home is bleak
rain appears from a clear blue sky
floodwaters roar all night
my sword remains by the Southern Dipper
my letters buffet the distant North Wind
I would send gifts of Changsha oranges
but who will take them to Loyang Bridge

66

宿龍興寺　綦毋潛

香剎夜忘歸　松清古殿扉
燈明方丈室　珠繫比丘衣
白日傳心淨　青蓮喻法微
天花落不盡　處處鳥銜飛

Ch'i-wu Ch'ien (692–749) was from the Yangtze city of Chiangling and served in Ch'ang-an as a censor and later as editorial director of the Palace Library. He was known for his well-crafted poems but better known for those written to him by others. Some commentators say this temple was 100 kilometers southwest of Chiangling near Lingling; others say it was 300 kilometers northeast near Fanghsien. Trees are planted outside a temple's main gate as guardians of the serenity within. The lamp of wisdom lights the abbot's chamber, where he gives personal instruction. Strands of beads are used for keeping track of repetitions of the Buddha's name, but a single bead was sometimes used to fasten a monk's robe. In any case, their simplicity contrasts with the attire of officials. The lotus represents the transcendent teaching of the Buddha that remains rooted in the mud of this world. In the *Vimalakirti Sutra*: 7, a celestial deity showers flowers on those who cultivate the Dharma. But the petals don't cling to those who are detached from their practice.

Spending the Night at Lunghsing Temple

CH'I-WU CH'IEN

> I failed to leave the temple by dark
> pine trees cooled the shrine-hall gate
> a lamp illumined the abbot's chamber
> beads held monastic robes together
> the white sun taught the purity of mind
> a blue lotus showed the subtlety of truth
> heavenly petals fell without cease
> everywhere birds carried them off

67

破山寺後禪院　常建

清晨入古寺　初日照高林
曲徑通幽處　禪房花木深
山光悅鳥性　潭影空人心
萬籟此俱寂　惟聞鐘磬音

Ch'ang Chien (708–765) grew up in Ch'ang-an but failed to gain an appointment in the capital and was assigned to provincial posts south of the Yangtze. Losing interest in the civil service, he took up wandering. Here, he visits a temple on Yushan, just outside the Yangtze Delta city of Changshu. The temple was later renamed Hsingfu Temple, and it was one of the country's major training monasteries during the T'ang and Sung dynasties. The temple is still there, and the path behind it still winds through a mixed forest of fruit trees and conifers. The "ten thousand noises" refer to those of the nearby urban world. The bell is used to mark the beginning and end of meditation periods as well as the time for meals and sleep. Talking during meditation retreats is restricted to instruction in the Dharma.

The Meditation Hall behind Poshan Temple

CH'ANG CHIEN

I entered an ancient temple at dawn
the rising sun lit the tall trees
a trail led off to a secluded place
to a meditation hall in a flowering wood
where mountain light pleased the hearts of birds
and pond reflections stilled men's minds
the ten thousand noises were hushed
all I heard was a bell

68

題松汀驛　張祐

山色遠含空　蒼茫澤國東
海明先見日　江白迴聞風
鳥道高原去　人煙小徑通
那知舊遺逸　不在五湖中

Chang Hu (792–852) was born in Hopei province but grew up in Suchou, next to Lake Taihu. When he later moved to Ch'ang-an to prepare for the civil service exam, he aroused the enmity of the powerful Hanlin academician Yuan Chen and was forced to leave town. He took this as a sign that an official career was not for him, and he built a cottage near Tanyang, where he spent the rest of his life. The Sungting relay station was apparently in the vicinity of the Yangtze and Lake Taihu, which was said to comprise five bodies of water and was also called Five Lakes. This region was famous as a place where a person could avoid the notice of the authorities, and it was the home of many bandits and martial arts heroes. The friends to whom Chang refers are those, like himself, who were forced into early retirement.

Written at the Sungting Relay Station

CHANG HU

Hill shapes merge with the far-off sky
east of the mist-covered marshlands
the ocean glows with the day's first light
the river turns white in the distant wind
steep trails lead to a high plateau
small paths link columns of smoke
why are all my retired friends
not here among the Five Lakes

69

聖果寺　釋處默

路自中峰上　盤回出薜蘿
到江吳地盡　隔岸越山多
古木叢青靄　遙天浸白波
下方城郭近　鐘磬雜笙歌

Ch'u-mo (fl. 850–900) was born in Shaohsing and became a monk when he was still a young man. Along with his hometown friend and fellow monk, Kuan-hsiu, he moved to Hangchou, and after several years both men headed up the Yangtze together. Ch'u-mo settled on Lushan, while Kuan-hsiu continued on to Chengtu. Prior to his departure, Ch'u-mo wrote this poem about the view from Shengkuo Temple at the summit of Fenghuangshan, outside Hangchou's South Gate. To the southeast, the Chientang River marked the border between the ancient states of Wu and Yueh (Ch'u-mo's homeland) as it flowed into Hangchou Bay. To the northwest was the city's West Lake, which was already a popular spot with revelers in the late T'ang dynasty (618–906).

Shengkuo Temple

Leading up from lesser peaks
the trail winds above vine-covered slopes
the land of Wu ends at the shore
the mountains of Yueh begin across the river
ancient trees merge with blue mist
the distant sky joins the white waves
the city wall is so close below
singers and flutes muffle the bell

70

野望
王績

東皋薄暮望
徙倚欲何依
樹樹皆秋色
山山惟落暉
牧人驅犢返
獵馬帶禽歸
相顧無相識
長歌懷采薇

Wang Chi (585–644) was from Shansi province and retired twice, the last time to Tungkao near his family home in Hochin. Tungkao means "Eastern Paddy" and appears as a place-name in a poem by T'ao Yuan-ming, on whose life of simplicity Wang modeled his own. Here, the cowherds remind him of the leaders of the new T'ang dynasty, and the hunters call to mind its generals. But watching them go by, he sees no friends and sings instead about the blameless pursuit of gathering ferns, just as the recluses Po-yi and Shu-ch'i did when they refused to serve King Wu (r. 1122–1116 B.C.), the founder of the Chou dynasty. Retiring to a mountain just south of Tungkao, they sang: "Climb that west slope / pick those ferns / trading evil for evil / don't they know is wrong / the sage kings are gone / where can we go / oh we're both finished / life doesn't last."

Gazing across the Countryside

WANG CHI

Watching dusk fade at Tungkao
I look for something to lean on
every tree is the color of fall
peak after peak loses its light
cowherds lead their calves home
hunters ride by with their prey
I look but don't know their faces
I sing about gathering ferns

71

送別崔著作東征　陳子昂

金天方肅殺　白露始專征
王師非樂戰　之子慎佳兵
海氣侵南部　邊風掃北平
莫賣盧龍塞　歸邀麟閣名

Ch'en Tzu-ang (661–702) was a censor at the court of Empress Wu, and Ts'ui Jung was editor of the court diary and calendar. In 696 Ts'ui was also assigned as court secretary to the army sent to pacify the Khitans. Dark skies of windblown loess are common in fall in North China, and "White Dew" is the name of a solar period in early September. A poem in the *Book of Odes* envisions the army as a tool for pacification rather than for war, and Lao-tzu says, "Fine swords aren't auspicious tools" (31). The fifth and sixth lines refer to areas of Hopei province, including the Pohai seacoast, occupied by the Khitans. Lulung Pass was just inside the Great Wall east of Beijing, and the walls of Unicorn Hall were covered with portraits of heroes by Emperor Hsuan (r. 73–49 B.C.).

Seeing Off Editor Ts'ui Marching East

CH'EN TZU-ANG

Golden skies have turned forbidding
white dew marks the start of your mission
the empress's armies don't enjoy war
her generals shun fine swords
but ocean storms trouble the South
and border winds sweep the North
don't sell out at Lulung Pass
or seek your fame at Unicorn Hall

72

陪諸貴公子丈八沟攜妓
納涼晚際遇雨（一）　杜甫

落日放船好　　輕風生浪遲
竹深留客處　　荷淨納涼時
公子調冰水　　佳人雪藕絲
片雲頭上黑　　應是雨催詩

Changpa Reservoir was located halfway between the southwest corner of Ch'ang-an and the nearby Chungnan Mountains, and supplied water to the capital via the Tungchi Canal. The scene is midsummer, when lotuses are in full bloom and a little relief from the heat is welcome. Ice was stored underground in straw-filled boxes during winter and sold to those who could afford it during the summer. Lotus roots are about the size of a yam. Once their thick skin is removed they are sliced and either stir-fried or, in this case, eaten raw and washed down with chilled rice wine.

Encountering Rain at Changpa Reservoir One Evening While Enjoying a Cool Breeze with Rich Young Men and Their Singsong Girls—1

TU FU

Sunset is just right for boating
a light breeze stirs a few waves
boaters pause by the dense bamboo
and breathe in the cool lotus-flower air
the young men add ice to their drinks
the women scrape lotus roots clean
a cloud overhead turns dark
surely the rain will bring poems

73

陪諸貴公子丈八沟攜妓
納涼晚際遇雨（二）　杜甫

雨來沾席上　風急打船頭
越女紅裙濕　燕姬翠黛愁
纜侵堤柳繫　幔卷浪花浮
歸路翻蕭颯　陂塘五月秋

Tu Fu's friends have hired a boat to take them out on the water but have now returned to the shore, soaked by the sudden downpour. The sitting mats were made of woven grass, and the awning was also woven, but probably from thin strips of bamboo or rattan. The women of the ancient states of Yueh in Southeast China and Yen in the Northeast were known for their beauty and also for their voices, and they were sought after as entertainers. The reservoir was about ten kilometers south of Ch'ang-an but only a few kilometers west of Tu Fu's home on the Tungling Plateau. At least he didn't have to travel as far as his rich young friends and their companions.

Encountering Rain at Changpa Reservoir One Evening While Enjoying a Cool Breeze with Rich Young Men and Their Singsong Girls—II

TU FU

Rain drenches the mats
wind beats against the prow
girls from Yueh wring out their red skirts
girls from Yen lament their mascara
even with the boat tied to a willow
the awning still lifts in the spray
the road home looks desolate now
on a fall day in May at the lake

74

宿雲門寺閣　孫逖

香閣東山下　煙花象外幽
懸燈千嶂夕　卷幔五湖秋
畫壁餘鴻雁　紗窗宿斗牛
更疑天路近　夢與白雲遊

Sun T'i (fl. 720) was a native of Shantung and served in several prominent posts in the capital, including the Secretariat. Here, while waiting to be recalled from an assignment in Chekiang province, he visits a Taoist temple at the foot of East Peak, fifteen kilometers south of Shaohsing. The Taoist immortal Wang Tzu-ch'iao was said to have lived here during the Han dynasty, and brightly colored clouds were often reported in its vicinity. Hence its name: Yunmen (Cloud Gate). As Sun looks south into the myriad peaks of the Kuaichi Range he feels the first cool air of autumn rising from the lake region to the north. Seeing the images of wild geese on the wall and, outside, two constellations that were associated with this region to which officials out of favor were banished, he dreams of returning to the capital, but apparently as an immortal.

Spending the Night at Yunmen Temple Pavilion

SUN T'I

At Incense Pavilion below East Peak
the flowers in the mist were from another world
I held up a lantern on a deep mountain night
and pulled back the curtain on a lakeland fall
the swans stayed behind on the walls
the Dipper and the Ox spent the night in the window
the road to Heaven seemed so close again
I dreamed I was traveling with clouds

75

秋登宣城謝脁北樓　李白

江城如畫裏　山晚望晴空
兩水夾明鏡　雙橋落彩虹
人煙寒橘柚　秋色老梧桐
誰念北樓上　臨風懷謝公

Hsieh T'iao (464–499) was known for his landscape poems and built this tower while serving as prefect of Hsuancheng, to which he had been sent at the urging of jealous officials at the Southern Ch'i (479–502) court in Nanching. Li Pai (701–762) also sees himself at the mercy of the T'ang court and combines his own sense of injustice with a landscape poem in Hsieh's honor. The tower was south of town on the slopes of Lingyang-shan and faced north toward two bridges that spanned one of the two rivers that circled the town. In the second line, some editions have *hsiao* (dawn) in place of *wan* (dusk), but Li Pai was never known for getting up early. The paulownia is a large-leafed shade tree that loses its leaves in early autumn.

Climbing Hsieh T'iao's North Tower in Hsuancheng in Autumn

LI PAI

This river town looks like a painting
mountains at dusk against a clear sky
two rivers frame an unblemished mirror
twin bridges form a rainbow
kitchen smoke and winter oranges
fall colors and leafless paulownias
who thinks of climbing North Tower
of facing the wind and remembering Hsieh T'iao

76

臨洞庭湖贈張丞相　孟浩然

八月湖水平　涵虛混太清
氣蒸雲夢澤　波撼岳陽城
欲濟無舟楫　端居恥聖明
坐觀垂釣者　徒有羨魚情

Meng Hao-jan (689–740) cultivated the life of a recluse but clearly harbored hopes of public service. He gave this poem to Chang Chiu-ling during a visit to Ch'ang-an in 733, shortly after Chang became prime minister. Once the high water of summer recedes, much of Tungting Lake becomes a marsh. Cloud Dream Marsh included two such sections of the western shore. Yuehyang is on the eastern shore and is still a major port for river traffic. Most commentators interpret the waves here as referring to the lake's water. But the lake is flat, and the only waves are those of the vapors that rise from the lake's broken hearts: Ch'u Yuan (340–278 B.C.) drowned himself in the Milo River just south of Yuehyang, and the two wives of Emperor Shun (c. 2250 B.C.) also drowned themselves near here and became the lake's resident spirits. In the last couplet, Meng recalls a story in *Huainantzu*: "Rather than covet the fish in the deeps, better to go home and make a good net" (17).

Overlooking Tungting Lake—For Prime Minister Chang

MENG HAO-JAN

In September the lake is so flat
the great hollow joins the celestial void
vapors rise from Cloud Dream Marsh
the waves rock Yuehyang walls
but there's no boat to take me across
and retirement is shameful in a golden age
sitting watching other people fish
to covet their catch is vain

77

過香積寺　王維

不知香積寺　數里入雲峰
古木無人徑　深山何處鐘
泉聲咽危石　日色冷青松
薄暮空潭曲　安禪制毒龍

Wang Wei (701–761) spent much of his time wandering in the mountains. Hsiangchi Temple was fifteen kilometers southwest of Ch'ang-an, on top of one of the plateaus formed by the loess that blew down from Mongolia in winter and settled at the foot of the Chungnan Mountains. The clouds on this occasion are below the plateau and envelop the capital. The temple was built around A.D. 700 at the confluence of the Hao and Chueh Rivers by the disciples of Shan-tao (d. 681), one of the patriarchs of Pure Land Buddhism. The serpent in the pool represents the delusions of the mind. For a comparison of Pure Land with Zen practice by the temple's recently-deceased abbot, see *Road to Heaven*, pg. 95.

Passing Hsiangchi Temple

WANG WEI

Unaware of Hsiangchi Temple
I walked for miles past mountains of clouds
ancient trees an empty path
somewhere in the hills a bell
streamsound murmuring boulders
the sun through cold green pines
a silent pool in fading light
where Zen subdued the serpent

送鄭侍御謫閩中　高適

謫去君無恨　閩中我舊過
大都秋雁少　只是夜猿多
東路雲山合　南天瘴癘和
自當逢雨露　行矣慎風波

Kao Shih (702–765) tries to mollify a friend being sent to Fukien as punishment for performing too well his job of criticizing breaches of policy and law. Geese are a reminder of exile, but they can fly north in spring. Kao would have us believe they don't fly as far south as Fukien. Still, one cannot avoid hearing the eerie howl of a gibbon and being reminded of one's desolation. The Coast Road skirts the East China Sea in Chekiang and Fukien. What Kao means by "the South" is "in this part of the South." Elsewhere in the South the climate was equivalent to a death sentence for Northerners. At the end of this poem Kao encourages his friend by trying to assure him that he will enjoy imperial favor (rain and dew), but only if he can avoid stirring up more trouble (wind and waves).

For Censor Cheng on Being Banished to Fukien

KAO SHIH

Go into exile but bear no grudge
I was once in Fukien myself
geese for the most part are rare in fall
though gibbons are common at night
the Coast Road merges with cloud-high peaks
but miasmas and plagues in the South are mild
you'll know the rain and dew again
go but watch out for the wind and waves

79

秦州雜詩　杜甫

鳳林戈未息　魚海路常難
候火雲峰峻　懸軍幕井乾
風連西極動　月過北庭寒
故老思飛將　何時議築壇

Tu Fu (712–770) wrote this poem in 759 after resigning his post near Huashan and moving briefly to Tienshui (Chinchou), before continuing on to Chengtu to escape the chaos that followed the An Lu-shan Rebellion. Fenglin and Yuhai were border posts west of Tienshui, under attack by the Turks. The Northern Court (Peiting) was the name of a major Chinese garrison that had already fallen on the Silk Road near Urumuchi. Signal towers burned straw at night and wolf dung, which emitted an intense black smoke, during the day. Li Kuang was a hero of China's earlier conquest of this region and was known as the Flying General. Tu Fu suggests placating his maligned spirit might help the country overcome its current crisis. The reference here is an oblique one to Kuo Tzu-yi, who defeated the armies of An Lu-shan but suffered the slander of jealous officials at court.

Miscellaneous Poem at Chinchou

TU FU

The fighting goes on in Fenglin
the road to Yuhai is still blocked
signal fires fill the sky with smoke
troops in the field find only dry wells
the wind shakes even the Western stars
the moon turns cold above the Northern Court
an old man recalls the Flying General
when will they build him an altar

80

禹廟空山裏　秋風落日斜
荒庭垂橘柚　古屋畫龍蛇
雲氣生虛壁　江聲走白沙
早知乘四載　疏鑿控三巴

禹廟　杜甫

After his patron died in 765, Tu Fu left Chengtu and headed down the Yangtze. Here, he stops outside Chunghsien at a shrine to Yu the Great. Yu founded the Hsia dynasty (c. 2200 B.C.) and was credited with taming China's rivers, not by building dikes but by dredging them. He is also credited with introducing the orange to Szechuan. But here his shrine has been neglected, and the fruit hangs unpicked, much like Tu Fu's own talents. It was said that Yu adapted himself to every situation: he rode chariots on land, boats on water, sledges on mudflats, and palanquins in the mountains. But Tu Fu has achieved no such mastery. The Land of Pa included the eastern half of Szechuan. It was the Pa (dragon) tribe that first settled this region.

Shrine to Yu the Great

TU FU

A shrine to Yu on a desolate slope
in autumn wind and the sun's last rays
a tree full of oranges in an overgrown courtyard
a dragon mural in an ancient hall
vapor rising from a rocky cliff
roar of the river scouring the sand
once he mastered the art of riding
he opened up this Land of Pa

81

望秦川　李頎

秦川朝望迥　日出正東峰
遠近山河淨　逶迤城闕重
秋聲萬戶竹　寒色五陵松
有客歸歟嘆　淒其霜露濃

Li Ch'i (690–751) served mostly in provincial posts but enjoyed a close association with a number of major poets in the capital. Here, he finally resigns and leaves for his home in Szechuan. Standing atop Ch'ang-an's north wall he sees the sun rising behind Lishan (a spur of the Chungnan Mountains to the east), the Wei River to the north (its watershed was also called the Valley of Ch'in, as the state of Ch'in once controlled this region), and the imperial grave mounds of Wuling to the northwest. He also hears the soughing of bamboo in the myriad palace gardens below. In the seventh line he recalls Confucius's regret in not finding anyone to employ his teachings and his anxiety that his disciples would not be able to pass them on (*Analects*: 5.21). The last line paraphrases the *Lichi* (*Book of Rites*): "When a gentleman walks on frost, sadness fills his heart" (24).

Gazing at the Valley of Ch'in

LI CH'I

Gazing at the Valley of Ch'in at dawn
the rising sun behind the east peak
mountains and rivers near and far so clear
undulating wall upon palace wall
the sound of autumn from a world of bamboo
the look of winter among Wuling pines
let's go home a traveler sighs
the frost and dew are so thick

同王徵君洞庭有懷　張謂

八月洞庭秋　瀟湘水北流
還家萬里夢　為客五更愁
不用開書帙　偏宜上酒樓
故人京洛滿　何日復同遊

Chang Wei (720–770) was a native of the Loyang area and served as a minor official in various posts in the central government. He wrote this poem in 747 during his rustication to Changsha, the capital of Hunan province, south of Tungting Lake. The title *cheng-chun* (gentleman-in-waiting) was an honorary epithet for someone who had been recommended to office, but it was not a formal position. Wang was thus exempt from the civil service exam ("no need to open a book") but was clearly still "waiting." Tungting Lake is fed by several rivers, but the largest is the Hsiang, which is joined near its source by the Hsiao. Chang watches their waters flow north through the lake, into the Yangtze, and toward Loyang, while he and his friend wait to be called back to the capital.

Commiserating with Gentleman-in-Waiting Wang on Tungting Lake

CHANG WEI

Through Tungting Lake in the middle of fall
the waters of the Hsiao and Hsiang flow north
but home is a thousand-mile dream away
and a guest greets dawn with sorrow
there's no need to open a book
far better to visit an inn
Ch'ang-an and Loyang are full of old friends
but when will we join them again

83

渡揚子江　丁仙芝

桂楫中流望　空波兩岸明
林開揚子驛　山出潤州城
海盡邊陰靜　江寒朔吹生
更聞楓葉下　淅瀝度秋聲

Ting Hsien-chih (fl. 713–741) was a native of this area where the Grand Canal crosses the Yangtze. He was known for his love of wine and travel and once served as military commander of Hangchou. Here, he takes the ferry south of Yangchou—it was this stretch between Yangchou and the sea that was called the Yangtze. On the south shore are Junchou (Chenchiang) and its temple-covered hills, and beyond Junchou is Tanyang, Ting's hometown. He has been away so long he can hear its leaves falling even in the middle of the river. Oars of *Cinnamomum cassia* represent virtue rebuffed. Ch'u Yuan (340–278 B.C.) used such oars in his failed rendezvous in "The Princess of the Hsiang." Ting's use of this metaphor suggests that he, too, considers his lord fickle.

Crossing the Yangtze

TING HSIEN-CHIH

My oars of cassia I gaze from midstream
the sky and waves and both shores are clear
the treeline parts at the Yangtze ferry
hills rise up from the Junchou walls
the edge of the sea is dark and silent
a chill wind comes from the river's cold
again I hear maple leaves falling
the brittle sounds of another autumn

84

幽州夜飲　張說

涼風吹夜雨　蕭瑟動寒林
正有高堂宴　能忘遲暮心
軍中宜劍舞　塞上重笳音
不作邊城將　誰知恩遇深

Chang Yueh (667–731) was sent, around 720, to serve as commander-in-chief at Yochou (an administrative area equivalent to that of modern Beijing, with its headquarters in Tahsing in the suburbs south of the present city); forces were stationed there to defend the empire against incursions by the nomadic Khitans. Chang had previously served as chief advisor to the emperor but had subsequently been demoted to a series of provincial posts and was uncertain whether this new post was a promotion or another demotion. Some commentators read the last couplet as an attempt to see it as a promotion. But such an assignment only serves to remind Chang how much he misses his family. Thus, while "grace" ostensibly refers to that of the emperor, it also refers to that of his wife and children. Ironically, Chang's ancestors were from Yuchou, and he would have found a warm welcome there. Still, the sixth line suggests homesickness rules the

Drinking at Night in Yuchou

CHANG YUEH

A cold wind fills the night with rain
and whistles through a leafless wood
attending a sumptuous banquet
we can forget old age
soldiers are fond of a sword dance
but favor the flute on the border
if I never served as a frontier general
how could I know the extent of grace

night. While the sword dance impresses with its flashy display, the sound of a flute travels farther and carries those who hear it back to those they miss — in Chang's case, to his home in Loyang.

PART THREE

85

春日偶成　程顥

雲淡風輕近午天　傍花隨柳過前川
時人不識余心樂　將謂偷閒學少年

Ch'eng Hao (1032–1085) was born near Hankou in Hupei province and grew up in Loyang. He and his younger brother, Ch'eng Yi, were major advocates of the neo-Confucian revival that dominated the intellectual life of the Sung dynasty. During the ten years he taught in Loyang, his students numbered in the thousands. He also served at the Sung capital in Kaifeng as a companion to the crown prince and as an investigating censor. But due to his opposition to the policies of Wang An-shih, he was demoted and sent to Chenning in Kuangsi province, where he served as an administrative assistant. He was later recalled but died on his way back. The third line recalls a story in *Chuangtzu* in which Chuang-tzu is out walking with Hui-tzu and pauses to comment on the joy of the fishes playing under a bridge. Hui-tzu says, "You're not a fish. How do you know if the fishes are happy?" The Taoist sage replied, "You're not me. How do you know I don't know the fishes are happy?" (17.13).

Casual Poem on a Spring Day

CH'ENG HAO

The clouds are thin the wind is light the sun is nearly overhead
past the flowers through the willows down along the stream
people don't see the joy in my heart
they think I'm wasting time or acting like a child

86

春日　朱熹

勝日尋芳泗水濱
無邊光景一時新
等閒識得東風面
萬紫千紅總是春

Chu Hsi (1130–1200) was born and died south of the Wuyi Mountains in Fukien province, although his family's ancestral home was in Kiangsi. He served in a number of posts, including senior compiler in the imperial archives and governor of several provinces, but he is better known for carrying on the work of the Ch'eng brothers in promoting the Sung dynasty's neo-Confucian revival. He also made lasting contributions in the areas of literature and history. Here, he visits a river just north of Confucius's hometown of Chufu in Shantung province. One day Confucius asked his disciples what they most desired. After several related their political ambitions, Tseng Hsi said, "In the last month of spring, when the new clothes are ready, I would like to go down to the river with a couple of students and perform the rites of spring." The Master sighed and said, "I'm with you" (*Analects*: 11.7). According to the conceptions that underlie the *Book of Changes*, spring begins in the East.

Spring Day

CHU HSI

Along the Ssu River it's a fine day for blossoms
the landscape is endless and suddenly new
I recognize the East Wind's familiar face
a thousand pinks and purples and everywhere spring

87

春宵　蘇軾

春宵一刻值千金
花有清香月有陰
歌管樓臺聲細細
鞦韆院落夜沈沈

Su Shih (1037–1101), aka Su Tung-p'o, was a native of Meishan in Szechuan province and one of the greatest poets, essayists, calligraphers, and personalities of the Sung dynasty. He also served in a number of high-level posts, although his opposition to the policies of Wang An-shih resulted in a brief imprisonment and several banishments, the last of which was to the southern borders of the empire. Not long after the death of his wife he was allowed to return, but he died within months of retiring to a piece of land he had bought earlier outside Changchou in Chekiang province. The swing is said to have arrived in China during the first millennium B.C. via one of the nomadic groups on the country's northern border. It still plays an important part in the harvest celebrations of such hilltribes as the Hani (Aini), along China's southwest border, where its ropes are often thirty or forty feet in length and it literally takes one's breath away.

Spring Night

SU SHIH

A spring night hour is worth a ton of gold
the pure scent of flowers the moon's pale light
music from the terrace finer than silk
swinging in the courtyard far into the night

88

城東早春　楊巨源

詩家清景在新春　綠柳纔黃半未勻
若待上林花似錦　出門俱是看花人

Yang Chu-yuan (755–820) was from Yungchi in Shansi. He served as vice-governor of the southern half of the same province and also as director of studies at the imperial university. The Chinese love to go looking for the first signs of spring, especially the blossoms of such fruit trees as the plum and the apricot. The Royal Woods (Shanglin) consisted of a large tract of pear and chestnut trees planted adjacent to the palace in Ch'ang-an during the Ch'in dynasty. They were expanded during the Han dynasty to well beyond the western suburbs. The Pa River, at the eastern edge of Ch'ang-an, was famous for its willow-lined banks. Yang suggests that the true connoisseur of spring is able to appreciate the willow's emerging golden catkins without feeling the need to wait for the more ostentatious show to come. In his commentary, Wang Hsiang says this also refers to recognizing men of talent before they become known.

Early Spring East of Town

YANG CHU-YUAN

The best time for a poet is when spring is new
when willows turn gold but not completely
if you wait until the Royal Woods look like brocade
the whole town will be out gawking at flowers

89

春夜　王安石

金爐香盡漏聲殘　翦翦輕風陣陣寒

春色惱人眠不得　月移花影上欄杆

Wang An-shih (1021–1086) was from Fuchou in Kiangsi province and became one of the most famous prime ministers in Chinese history. His financial policies, however, resulted in a profound split among government officials and also in Wang's retirement to the hills east of Nanching. He wrote this poem in the spring of 1069, the year before he became prime minister. Spring marks the beginning of the agricultural calendar, and the reforms he was hoping to implement were primarily aimed at helping farmers. Hence, Wang has stayed up all night anticipating the new year. But the only flowers he sees are the shadow flowers on the railing outside his window. Sticks of incense and devices that dripped water were used to keep time during the night. The last three lines paraphrase lines in poems by Han Wo (844–923), Lo Yin (833–909), and Yao Ho (fl. 831).

Spring Night

WANG AN-SHIH

The burner is out of incense the dripping has almost stopped
the wind comes in gusts the cold in waves
springtime disturbs me and keeps me from sleep
the moon casts shadow flowers on the balustrade

90

初春小雨　韓愈

天街小雨潤如酥　草色遙看近卻無
最是一年春好處　絕勝煙柳滿皇都

Han Yu (768–824) was a native of Menghsien in Honan province. Although he spent a good part of his life serving in the upper echelons of government, he was banished on several occasions, most famously for his suggestion that the emperor's veneration of the Buddha's finger-bone would shorten his life. He was also a distinguished literary figure of the T'ang and its most ardent supporter of Confucian ideals. This was written in 823 shortly before his death and was the first of two poems he wrote on the appointment of his friend Chang Chi, entitled "For Chang Shih-pa [the eighteenth son], Vice-Director of the Bureau of Waterways and Irrigation, in Early Spring." The "streets of Heaven" and the "royal city" refer to Ch'ang-an, the residence of the Son of Heaven. Here, the angle of view condenses the faint colors on the horizon, whereby green appears in the distance but not nearby, and the myriad new willow catkins look like so much mist.

Light Rain in Early Spring

HAN YU

The streets of Heaven glisten from light rain
grass appears far off but not nearby
this is truly the best time of spring
when the sight of misty willows fills the royal city

91

元旦　王安石

爆竹聲中一歲除
春風送暖入屠蘇
千門萬戶曈曈日
總把新桃換舊符

Wang An-shih (1021–1086) wrote this poem soon after being appointed prime minister in 1070 and beginning implementation of his controversial agricultural reforms. Hence, while he records customs associated with the lunar New Year, he also has his new policies in mind. The Chinese viewed the year as a spirit named *Nien* (Year), which needed to be encouraged to make way for its replacement. In ancient times the Chinese heated sections of bamboo that chased the Year away when they exploded. During the Sung these were replaced by paper tubes filled with a new concoction — gunpowder. In preparation for the New Year the Chinese still steep a combination of herbs in grain alcohol during the winter. This combination (called *Tusu*) includes cinnamon, pepper, *Atractylis lancea*, *Siler divaricatum*, and balloon flower root. According to the T'ang-dynasty herbalist Sun Ssu-miao, drinking Tusu wine on New Year's Day drives off infections. Because *t'ao* (peach) was a homophone of *t'ao* (chase away), the

New Year's Day

WANG AN-SHIH

Firecracker sounds chase the Year away
spring wind infuses herbal wine with warmth
outside countless doorways in the rising sun
new peach prints are pasted over last year's charms

wood of the peach tree was thought to have the power of exorcising evil
spirits and was used to make the block prints of guardians and sages that
were pasted outside doorways on New Year's Day. These prints originated
just south of Kaifeng in Chuhsienchen, which became one of the world's
first centers of printing in the tenth and eleventh centuries.

92

上元侍宴　蘇軾

淡月疏星遠建章　仙風吹下御爐香

侍臣鵠立通明殿　一朵紅雲捧玉皇

This was one of three poems Su Shih (1037–1101) wrote at imperial request while attending a dawn banquet for court officials on the occasion of Shangyuan (the Great Beginning), which celebrates the first full moon of the year, when the moon sinks in the west at dawn prior to its return at sunset for Yuanhsiao (Lantern Festival). But the sinking moon and fading stars also represent Wang An-shih and his supporters at court, whose policies Su opposed and whose light pales in the glory of the imperial presence. Chienchang Court was built during the Han dynasty as part of the palace in Ch'ang-an, but here it refers to the assembled officials in the Sung capital of Kaifeng. Tungming Palace is where Yu Huang-ti (the Jade Emperor/Sage on High) resides in the highest of the Taoist heavens. But here the palace is in Kaifeng, rather than the heavens, and the sage is the Sung emperor. In honor of the occasion, officials wore red robes, the color of life. Standing in the courtyard perfectly still and *en masse*, they resembled the horizon at dawn.

Attending a Banquet on the Great Beginning

SU SHIH

Pale moon and scattered stars encircle Chienchang Court
celestial winds waft incense from the royal censer
inside Tungming Palace officials stand like storks
an offering of red clouds for the Sage on High

93

立春偶成　張栻

律回歲晚冰霜少　春到人間草木知

便覺眼前生意滿　東風吹水綠參差

Chang Shih (1133–1180) was born in Mienchu in Szechuan province and later moved to Hengyang in Hunan. The son of the famous general and prime minister, Chang Chun, he served in the Southern Sung capital of Hangchou and eventually reached the post of senior compiler of the dynastic history. He was also known for his essays advocating Confucian values. Chang, Chu Hsi, and Lu Tsu-ch'ien were ranked as the three illuminati of their age. The Arrival of Spring (*Lichun*) is a solar period that begins shortly after the lunar New Year, usually in the first week of February. The division of the year into phases of light and dark, or *yin* and *yang*, goes back to the Yellow Emperor. In the ancient system of trigrams devised by Fu Hsi around 2800 B.C. and reworked by King Wen around 1100 B.C., east is the direction of spring and west is the direction of autumn. In the different but complementary systems of these two men, east is also seen as the direction of either fire or thunder, while west is the location of water or lakes.

Occasional Poem on the Arrival of Spring

CHANG SHIH

The light is back the year is past ice and frost are rare
plants and trees all know spring is in the world
we see the force of life spread before our eyes
the East Wind blowing water ripples green

94

打毬圖　晁說之

閶闔千門萬戶開　三郎沈醉打毬回

九齡已老韓休死　無復明朝諫疏來

Ch'ao Yueh-chih (1059–1129) was from Chuyeh in Shantung province and served as a member of the Hanlin Academy in Kaifeng, where he was assigned the task of recording imperial pronouncements during the emperor's morning meeting with his officials, which apparently inspired this poem. Ch'ao was also known for his skill as a painter, and here he portrays Emperor Hsuan-tsung (685–762), the third son of Emperor Jui-tsung (662–716), indulging in a game similar to soccer that employed a leather ball stuffed with feathers — while the country went to ruin. At the beginning of Hsuan-tsung's reign his chief ministers, Chang Chiu-ling and Han Hsiu, submitted memorials criticizing his lack of attention to governmental affairs. But both were eventually forced to resign or retire and thereafter the emperor seldom received frank advice, much less criticism, during his dawn audience. Ch'ao could only have written this poem about an emperor of a previous dynasty, but his reference is clearly to Emperor

On a Painting of Playing Football

CH'AO YUEH-CHIH

A thousand doors and windows open in the palace
the Third Son is drunk and gives the ball a kick
Chiu-ling is too old and Han Hsiu is dead
no longer are memorials submitted in the morning

Hui-tsung (r. 1101–1126), whose passion for the arts and whose inattention
to governmental affairs are blamed for the loss of North China to the
Khitans and for the flight of the court from Kaifeng to Hangchou, where
his successors established the Southern Sung dynasty (1127–1279).

95

太平天子朝元日　五色雲車駕六龍
金殿當頭紫閣重　仙人掌上玉芙蓉

宮詞（一）　林洪

Lin Hung (fl. 1250) was a native of Fukien province, but little else is known about him. One source says he was a seventh-generation descendant of the Hangchou recluse Lin Pu (967–1028). This and the following poem are from a series of one hundred verses written by the poet on life in the palace in Hangchou. On New Year's Day the Chinese pay respects to their ancestors. And since the emperor is the Son of Heaven he greets his progenitors in semimythical fashion, reminiscent of the ascent of his shaman predecessors during their annual communion with ancestral spirits. At the palace in Hangchou there were two pillars, on top of which stood two immortals offering up jade lotuses to the gods. The flowers also served the function of collecting dew unsullied by earthly dust. The dew was then used in elixirs. A number of commentators point to this and to the following poem as examples of the lower standards used by the compiler in including a handful of poems by friends, and they are deleted in some

Palace Ode—1

LIN HUNG

Above the gilded hall's purple-tiered pavilion
immortals offer up lotuses of jade
the Emperor of Peace greets the New Year dawn
his chariot of colored clouds drawn by dragon steeds

editions. Among those editions that include them, several incorrectly attribute them to Wang Chien (751–830), who also wrote a series of one hundred poems on palace life in the T'ang. In ancient times, horses over seven feet tall were called "dragon steeds."

宮詞（二）　林洪

殿上衮衣明日月　硯中旗影動龍蛇
縱橫禮樂三千字　獨對丹墀日未斜

The poet describes the examination of candidates seeking appointment as officials, all of whom are required to write three-thousand-word essays according to forms established in the canons of ritual and prosody. Meanwhile, the emperor looks on, wearing a robe embroidered with images and symbols of the sun and moon. The Chinese make their ink by grinding sticks of soot and pine resin on flat stones, onto which small amounts of water are added. When the proper consistency is reached the ink is drained into a depression at one end of the stone. Here, the flapping banners hanging from the rafters are reflected in these pools of ink. Finally done, the candidates stand before the court's cinnabar-colored steps and present their work.

Palace Ode—*II*

LIN HUNG

At court the royal robes reflect the sun and moon
banner shadows move like dragons on the inkstones
the length and breadth of rites and music in three thousand words
line the cinnabar steps before the sun goes down

97

詠華清宮　杜常

行盡江南數十程　曉雲殘月入華清
朝元閣上西風急　都入長楊作雨聲

Tu Ch'ang (fl. 1080) was a descendant of Empress Chao-hsien (fl. 950) and held a series of midlevel posts in and around Kaifeng. Here, he visits the ruins of Huaching Palace (destroyed in 755 by An Lu-shan) east of Ch'ang-an, and he likens his journey to that of the relay riders who brought lychees from South China for Hsuan-tsung's favorite concubine, Yang Kuei-fei. The palace at Lishan was where the two lovers spent much of their time, while the T'ang dynasty went to ruin. Overlooking this testament to indulgence was Chaoyuan (Sunrise) Pavilion at the summit of Lishan. Normally, the West Wind indicates the coming of autumn in China. But west of Hanku Pass it means rain. The tall willows (ch'ang-yang) are interpreted by some as referring to the former Han-dynasty palace of that name, west of Ch'ang-an. But Huaching was also known for these trees, and it seems unlikely that the poet would have confused the two places, which were fifty kilometers apart. This was apparently written

In Praise of Huaching Palace

TU CH'ANG

A journey of countless stages from the Southland ends
with the pale moon and dawn clouds of Huaching
and the West Wind rushing past Sunrise Pavilion
entering the tall willows it sounds like rain

while Tu was traveling west to Tienshui to take up his post as senior judge
for the province, and he is concerned that his in-laws back at the Sung
capital might not have learned the lesson that Hsuan-tsung learned too
late. With some trepidation, I have amended the second line, reading
hsiao-yun (dawn clouds) for *hsiao-feng* (dawn wind) to avoid redundancy
in the third line.

98

清平調　李白

雲想衣裳花想容　春風拂檻露華濃
若非群玉山頭見　會向瑤臺月下逢

Li Pai (701–762) was born in Tokmak in what is now Kyrgyzstan and moved to Szechuan when he was five. After failing to secure a post through normal channels, he was given a sinecure at the Hanlin Academy in 742 based on his reputation as a poet. A year or so later, when he was drinking one day with friends, he was summoned to the palace, where Hsuan-tsung and Yang Kuei-fei were enjoying the peony blossoms. Asked to compose a few verses to the tune of "Chingping," he complied with this ode to erotic beauty and two other poems. However, he was so drunk he aroused the enmity of the eunuch, Kao Li-shih, who had to help him take off his boots and to grind his ink. Yang Kuei-fei also became incensed after Kao interpreted allusions in the other two poems as referring to women who brought the country to ruin. Li Pai was soon sent packing and never returned to the capital. The jade peaks are in the land of immortals, and Alabaster Terrace is at the court of Hsi-wang-mu (Queen Mother of the West), dispenser of the elixir of immortality.

Chingping Ode

LI PAI

Her cloudlike clothing and flowerlike face
spring wind at the threshold caresses her dewy luster
if this isn't a scene from the land of jade peaks
it must be Alabaster Terrace in the moonlight

99

題邸間壁　鄭會

酴釀香夢怯春寒　翠掩重門燕子閒

敲斷玉釵紅燭冷　計程應說到常山

Cheng Hui (fl. 1210) was a minor poet of the Sung about whom we know next to nothing. He wrote this poem in his wife's voice while traveling from Hangchou to Kiangsi province, probably at an inn in Changshan. Changshan was a major stop on the post road that led southwest from the Southern Sung capital. Cheng's home was in Kueihsi, still another 150 kilometers away. The variety of climbing raspberry he imagines in his wife's dream, *Rubus rosifolius* var. *commersonii*, blooms in this region at the end of spring. Swallows represent conjugal bliss but they, too, are waiting for warmer weather. The green is that of early spring foliage. Red candles are used for weddings, New Year's, and any other happy occasion. Women often used their hairpins as scissors to trim candle wicks, but here they lie broken from overuse. In some editions this poem is attributed to Cheng Ku (fl. 890–930), a prominent poet of the independent state of Nanping. Nanping controlled the area of the Yangtze east of the Three Gorges during the Five Dynasties Period (907–960) between the T'ang and Sung.

Written on the Wall of an Inn

CHENG HUI

A raspberry-scented dream dispels the chill of spring
the swallows are resting behind doors shrouded green
my jade hairpins lie broken the red candles are cold
according to my count he should be in Changshan

100

絕句　杜甫

兩個黃鸝鳴翠柳
一行白鷺上青天
窗含西嶺千秋雪
門泊東吳萬里船

Tu Fu (712–770) wrote this poem in the early summer of 764 while he and his family were living in Szechuan in a thatched cottage on a minor side-stream of the Min River, just outside the west wall of the provincial capital of Chengtu. Orioles are the harbingers of spring, as egrets are of summer. To the west of Chengtu are the Min Mountains, which formed the country's border with Tibet and which included peaks in excess of 6,000 meters. The Min River flowed out of the mountains and past Chengtu and connected Western Szechuan, via the Yangtze, with the rest of China. Tu Fu may have been living in relative security far from the chaos of North China, but he is already thinking of leaving. A few kilometers southeast of his house was Ten Thousand Mile Bridge, where Chu-ko Liang (181–234) bid goodbye to an emissary heading for Chekiang province with the words, "a journey of ten thousand miles begins right here." When Tu Fu's

Quatrain

TU FU

A pair of golden orioles sings in green willows
a column of snowy egrets flies off in blue sky
my window contains peaks with a thousand years of ice
my gate harbors boats from ten thousand miles downriver

patron died the following year, the poet and his family began their own
journey down the Min and Yangtze Rivers in search of another sanctuary.
This was the third in a series of four poems.

101

海棠　蘇軾

東風嫋嫋泛崇光　香霧空濛月轉廊
只恐夜深花睡去　故燒高燭照紅粧

Su Shih (1037–1101) was from Meishan in Szechuan province. Along with his father and younger brother, he was ranked among the eight greatest essayists of the T'ang and Sung dynasties. He was equally famous for his calligraphy and poetry and also served at the highest levels of government. But his opposition to the policies of Wang An-shih led to repeated banishments and even a brief imprisonment. Here, the East Wind represents the arrival of spring, and this harbinger of the season reminds Su of Yang Kuei-fei, concubine of Emperor Hsuan-tsung, who called her his "begonia." On one occasion she got so drunk that she slept for two nights. Hence, Su hopes to see her garden incarnation before she retires. Su wrote this poem at the beginning of his banishment to Huangchou, down the Yangtze from Wuhan, at a garden known for its begonias.

Begonia

SU SHIH

The East Wind gently spreads her celestial glow
the moon slips behind her veil of perfumed mist
afraid this flower won't stay up much longer
I light a tall candle to view her crimson face

102

清明　杜牧

清明時節雨紛紛
路上行人欲斷魂
借問酒家何處有
牧童遙指杏花村

Tu Mu (803–852) was born in Ch'ang-an to a once-prominent family that had lost its wealth and power by the time he was a boy. Hence, he grew up in poverty and began his studies relatively late. Still, he excelled in the literary arts and served in a number of posts, though of ever-decreasing importance. When he wrote this poem he was serving south of Nanching as prefect of Kueichih, and found himself far from home on a day in early April when family members make every effort to return to honor their deceased parents and ancestors. Since ancient times, Grave Sweeping Day (Chingming) has been the day when the Chinese pay their respects at their ancestral graves and cut back the weeds that have grown up since their last visit. The weather during this time of year is usually fine in North China, but not along the Yangtze. Still, this traveler is in luck. Apricot Blossom Village (Hsinghuatsun) was just west of Kueichih and was famous throughout China for its rice wine. The well that supplied the water is still there.

Grave Sweeping Day

TU MU

On Grave Sweeping Day the rain pours down
a traveler on the road feels his heart sink
where he asks can he buy some wine
a herdboy points off to Apricot Blossom Village

103

清明　王禹偁

無花無酒過清明　興味蕭然似野僧

昨日鄰家乞新火　曉窗分與讀書燈

Wang Yu-ch'eng (954–1001) was from Chuyeh in Shantung province. Although he was quite poor as a youth, he was recommended to the court by a local official and served in a series of posts that alternated between the highest and lowest echelons. While serving as a censor he was known for his forthright criticism of government policies and was eventually banished to the South. According to an ancient tradition, people were forbidden to eat hot food for the two days before Chingming, when families paid their respects at ancestral graves and made offerings of wine and flowers. After two days of cold hearths, people made a new fire by drilling willow wood. Here, the poet is so poor he has to borrow a light from his neighbor. However, he borrows it so that he can study before dawn in preparation for the civil service exams. In many ways the life of a would-be official was not unlike that of a poor monk who begs for his living. And yet, despite his poverty, the poet honors his ancestors with his diligence and willingness to suffer on behalf of the family name.

Chingming

WANG YU-CH'ENG

Celebrating Chingming without flowers or wine
bereft of excitement like a monk in the wilds
last night I begged a neighbor for new fire
for my lamp by the window to read before dawn

社日　王駕

鵝湖山下稻田肥
豚柵雞栖對掩扉
桑柘影斜春社散
家家扶得醉人歸

Wang Chia (851–890) was from near Yungchi in Shansi province and reached the post of vice-director of one of the bureaus in the Ministry of Rites in Ch'ang-an. Here, he is in Kiangsi province serving as prefect of Yenshan. Gooselake Mountain (Ohushan) was a few kilometers southeast of town. During the following century it was the location of a major Confucian academy. In ancient times the Chinese held a neighborhood festival in honor of the Earth God; it included twenty-five families and was held twenty-five days after the beginning of spring and fall. In the first line I have read *tao-t'ien fei* (fields are fertilized — therefore, ready) in place of *tao-liang-fei* (grain is fat). This emendation seems inescapable, as grain could not possibly be *fei* (fat) a month after New Year. On the other hand, *fei* was commonly used to describe fields. The closed sties and coops suggest that sows have just given birth and chicks have just hatched, and that they are being protected from predators in a family's absence. Mulberry

Festival Day

WANG CHIA

The fields below Gooselake Mountain are ready
the pigsties and chicken coops are all shut tight
mulberry shadows mean springfest is over
families all help their drunken men home

trees supply the leaves silkworms feed on. They are pruned in winter and put forth new leaves about this time, at least enough to cast shadows in the setting sun. Taxes were usually paid in silk; hence, this was a major concern of every family. Some editions attribute this poem to Chang Yen (fl. 880).

105

寒食　韓翃

春城無處不飛花
寒食東風御柳斜
日暮漢宮傳蠟燭
輕煙散入五侯家

Han Hung (fl. 750–780) was a native of Nanyang in Honan province. Although he served in midlevel posts in the capital, he was far better known for his poetry and was ranked as one of the Ten Talents of the Tali Period (766–779). One day when the chief minister informed Emperor Te-tsung that there was an opening in the Secretariat, the emperor said, "Give the post to Han Hung." The minister replied, "But there are two Han Hungs. Which one does his majesty mean?" Te-tsung said, "The one who wrote 'The city in spring isn't safe from flying petals.'" Although nowadays this poem is read as a critique of the privileged class, the emperor read it as a praise of imperial largesse. As noted in the commentary to verse 103, during the two days before Grave Sweeping Day no hot food was eaten. This observance was said to have begun 2,600 years ago with Duke Wen of the state of Chin, to commemorate the death of Chieh Chih-t'ui, who refused to come out of seclusion to serve at the Duke's court. Furious at Chieh's

Cold Food

HAN HUNG

The city in spring isn't safe from flying petals
on Cold Food Day before the East Wind royal willows lean
candles are sent from palace halls at sunset
smoke curls faintly inside the great estates

refusal, the Duke ordered the mountain on which Chieh lived burned.
Chieh still refused to come down and died in the fire. Here, too, the poet
notes the imperial custom, begun by Han-dynasty emperors, of sending
lighted candles to the rich and powerful, who were thus allowed to ignore
the ban on fire.

106

江南春　杜牧

千里鶯啼綠映紅
水村山郭酒旗風
南朝四百八十寺
多少樓臺煙雨中

Tu Mu (803–852) summarizes the sights of a journey through a region the Chinese call Chiangnan (South of the Yangtze) — to which he was rusticated from 838 to 842. Not only does this region south of the river's lower reaches enjoy a milder climate and more rainfall than North China, it was also more hospitable to mercantile activities and Buddhism during a series of southern dynasties (420–589). The Yangtze remains China's greatest highway, and from its river towns and hillside hamlets wineshops and inns advertised their presence with pennants suspended from bamboo poles. Emperor Wu of the Liang dynasty (502–556) was said to have built nearly 500 temples in this region, and Buddhist architecture was as much a part of the landscape as bamboo and lotuses. Thus, as he describes the sights and sounds, Tu Mu also suggests the reasons for the decline in dynastic fortunes: indulgence in worldly passions and the emptying of imperial coffers to support the otherworldly way of life of Buddhist monasteries. Pagodas usually contained the ashes and relics of eminent monks.

Chiangnan Spring

TU MU

A thousand miles of oriole songs and red among the green
of wine flags flapping along the shore and in the hills
four hundred and eighty temples built by the Southern Court
and how many pagodas in the land of mist and rain

107

上高侍郎　高蟾

天上碧桃和露種　日邊紅杏倚雲栽

芙蓉生在秋江上　不向東風怨未開

Kao Ch'an (fl. 850–890) grew up in Tsangchou near the mouth of the Yellow River and moved to Ch'ang-an as a young man. Although he became well known for his poetry, he had to take the civil service exam several times before finally succeeding in 876. Still, he eventually reached the post of deputy chief censor. Here, he compares those who enjoy imperial favor (dew and clouds) to varieties of fruit trees known for their blossoms, and he likens himself and his friend, Kao Pin, to the lotus that will have its day —but in late summer or early fall, not in spring when the East Wind blows. Kao Ch'an wrote this poem following one of his earlier failures to pass the civil service exam, when he learned his friend had been appointed military commissioner of the Huainan region, which was known for its lotuses. Hence, this poem is about the poet's own disappointment rather than about Kao Pin's. The second line was later quoted as part of a couplet in the Ming-dynasty novel *Dream of the Red Chamber*.

For Gentleman-in-Attendance Kao

KAO CH'AN

The green peach of heaven thrives in the dew
the red apricot of the sun flourishes by the clouds
the lotus that rises from a river in fall
doesn't blame the East Wind for not blooming sooner

108

古木陰中繫短篷　杖藜扶我過橋東

沾衣欲濕杏花雨　吹面不寒楊柳風

絕句　僧志安

Chih-nan (fl. 1200) was a Buddhist monk who lived near the foot of the Tientai Mountains at Kuoching Temple. A friend of many literati of his day, he was also responsible for publishing the first printed edition of the poems of Han-shan (Cold Mountain) in 1184. In this poem he describes a scene reminiscent of the fisherman who tied up his boat and traced peach blossoms floating down the stream back through a crevice in the rocks to the lost world immortalized by T'ao Yuan-ming in "Peach Blossom Spring." Here, apricot blossoms replace those of the peach. The fisherman, too, is replaced by an old monk who needs the help of a walking staff of *Chenopodium album* but whose spirit is invigorated by the spring weather. East is where the sun rises and is the direction associated with spring. The famous front gate of Kuoching Temple also faces east. Just past the gate is Fengkan Bridge, and beyond the bridge is the road (or trail in Chih-nan's day) that leads up the mountain.

Quatrain

CHIH-NAN

I tied up my sampan in the shade of an ancient tree
and headed east across the bridge with the help of my pigweed staff
my clothes were soaked by the apricot-blossom rain
but my face wasn't numbed by the willow-catkin wind

109

遊小園不值　葉紹翁

應嫌屐齒印蒼苔　十扣柴扉久不開
春色滿園關不住　一枝紅杏出牆來

Yeh Shao-weng (fl. 1200–1250) was from Lishui near the southern border of Chekiang province. Little else is known about him, other than that he served as an academician in the imperial archives in Hangchou and wrote in the unadorned style advocated by the Rivers and Lakes school of poetry. The Chinese often use moss as a ground cover in their gardens, and the clogs, which the Japanese still wear at home and at public baths, had two high wooden ridges on the bottom, one in front and one in back. The front ridge helped when going uphill, the back ridge when going downhill. And together they kept one's feet above the mud. The red blossoms are those of the apricot. The last line is quite famous but was originally part of an earlier poem by Lu Yu (1125–1210) entitled "Written on Horseback." There is also a nearly identical poem by Chang Liang-ch'en, a fellow member of the Rivers and Lakes school of poetry, entitled "Occasional Poem," but it's impossible to tell who is quoting whom. A variant of the second

Visiting a Private Garden without Success

YEH SHAO-WENG

It must be because he hates clogs on his moss
I knocked ten times still his gate stayed closed
but spring can't be kept locked in a garden
a branch of red blossoms reached past the wall

line reads: "I knocked ten times, nine times without success." But that
would suggest the owner finally opened his gate, which would seem at
odds with the title as well as with the last couplet. Another variant has "I
knocked lightly, but his gate stayed closed." But why lightly? Finally, some
editions attribute this poem to Yeh Shih (1150–1223).

110

客中行　李白

蘭陵美酒鬱金香　玉碗盛來琥珀光
但使主人能醉客　不知何處是他鄉

Li Pai (701–762) wrote this poem around 740 while visiting the sites associated with the founders of the Confucian tradition in Shantung province. In addition to paying his respects at the graves of Confucius and Mencius in Chufu and Tsouhsien, he also traveled to Lanling near the southeastern border of Shantung. This was the location of the grave of Hsun-tzu (third century B.C.), who is credited with establishing the teachings of Confucius at court. Lanling was also known for a wine infused with turmeric, or *Curcuma longa*, which was fragrant and reddish yellow in color and which was mixed with the wine drunk on ceremonial occasions during Confucius's day. To establish their reputations and connections, poets did quite a bit of traveling. Thus, much of Chinese poetry is dominated by the sentiments associated with being away from home.

Traveling Away from Home

LI PAI

The fine wine of Lanling with its turmeric scent
fills jade cups with its amber light
if only a host can keep his guests drunk
they'll soon forget about their hometowns

111

題屏　劉季孫

呢喃燕子語梁間　底事來驚夢裏閒
說與旁人渾不解　杖藜攜酒看芝山

Liu Chi-sun (fl. 1070) was born in the Sung capital of Kaifeng, but he spent most of his career as a minor official in the provinces. He wrote this poem in Kiangsi province while serving as inspector of the government winery in the town of Poyang on the eastern shore of Poyang Lake. Officials seldom took their families with them to their provincial posts, and the swallows, which represent marital harmony, remind Liu of his wife. Finding no sympathy at work, Liu decided to take the day off and left this memento for his fellow officials. Mushroom Mountain (Chihshan) was just north of town and represents the call of reverie, in which he finds solace from his sense of separation. One day not long after Liu wrote this, Wang An-shih (1021–1086) was serving as judicial commissioner for the same region and saw this poem on a screen in the office while checking for irregularities at the winery. He was so taken by the poem, he left without making an inspection. As a result, Liu enjoyed a brief moment of fame in

Written on a Screen

LIU CHI-SUN

Twittering swallows gossip in the rafters
why do they disturb my daydream reverie
the clerk beside me shrugs when I ask
I grab my staff and jug and head for Mushroom Mountain

literary circles, and though he was too honest to capitalize on it, he became deputy director of the Crafts Institute and later prefect of Hsihsien in Shansi province. When he died, the only property he left was a collection of thirty thousand books and several hundred paintings.

112

漫興　杜甫

腸斷春江欲盡頭　杖藜徐步立芳洲
顛狂柳絮隨風舞　輕薄桃花逐水流

This was the fifth in a series of nine poems Tu Fu (712–770) wrote in the late spring of 761. He was living on the bank of a minor branch of the Min River, just beyond the west gate of Chengtu, in a thatched cottage that sheltered him and his family during one of the few idyllic periods of his life. The second line recalls the end of Ch'u Yuan's "Lady of the Hsiang" in the *Chutzu*: "Sweet pollia I've picked on the flowering shore / to give to the maiden who lies below [one of the wives of Emperor Shun, who drowned herself in the Hsiang River] / what is gone cannot be found again / let us then wander and enjoy what is left." The petals recall T'ao Yuan-ming's story of a fisherman who sees peach blossoms floating down a stream and traces them upstream through a cleft in the rocks to an idyllic paradise untouched by the chaotic world of his time. Tu Fu feels that the hope of reaching such a paradise, illusory or not, has once again faded with the end of another spring—and how many springs does he have left?

Inspired

TU FU

The heartbreaking flood of spring is nearly over
I poke along with my staff and stand on a flowering shore
willow catkins dance wildly in the wind
peach petals float diaphanous in the current

113

慶全庵桃花　謝枋得

尋得桃源好避秦　桃紅又是一年春
花飛莫遣隨流水　怕有漁郎來問津

Hsieh Fang-te (1226–1289), aka Hsieh Ping-te, was from Yiyang in Kiangsi province and served in Hangchou as an examiner of civil service candidates. His selection of topics, however, led to his dismissal and subsequent demotion to the provinces, and eventually to the prefecture next to his hometown. When the Mongols finally brought the Southern Sung dynasty to an end in 1279, Hsieh formed an army of resistance in Yiyang, but he was defeated and fled to Fukien. He was later captured and taken to the new capital in Beijing, but he starved himself in prison rather than serve the rulers of the new Yuan dynasty. Here, he visits a hermitage in the hills just south of Yiyang. T'ao Yuan-ming's story, which supplies the background for this poem, recounts how a fisherman followed peach petals that were drifting down a stream until he reached their source in a cleft in the rocks. Squeezing through the crevice he came out into an idyllic valley, where he met people whose ancestors had come there several hundred years earlier

The Peach Blossoms of Chingchuan Hermitage

HSIEH FANG-TE

In Peach Blossom Valley they escaped the Ch'in
peach blossom red means spring is here again
don't let flying petals fall into the stream
some fisherman I fear might try to find their source

to escape the brutal rule of the Ch'in dynasty (221–207 B.C.). After returning to tell others of his discovery, the fisherman was unable to relocate the valley, as the refugees had obscured the trail and the crevice. Hsieh uses the Ch'in here to represent the Yuan (1280–1368), from whose encroaching dominion he hoped to find refuge.

114

玄都觀桃花　劉禹錫

紫陌紅塵拂面來　無人不道看花回
玄都觀裏桃千樹　盡是劉郎去後栽

Liu Yu-hsi (772–842) was a native of Loyang and a prominent, though often banished, poet. He wrote this poem in 815 upon returning to Ch'ang-an after a ten-year banishment to Hunan for siding with the reform faction of Wang Shu-wen. The combination of allusions in this poem — the purple (i.e., royal) paths of the imperial city, the red dust (of illusion and sensory indulgence), the name of the temple (*hsuan-tu* — celestial capital), the thousands of officials promoted since his banishment, and the thinly veiled reference to himself — together resulted in a second banishment. When he returned he wrote the next poem (verse 115) after visiting the same temple, and was banished for a third time. The Taoist temple to which he refers was just outside Ch'ang-an, and the people he meets are on their way back from going to see its blossoms. The peach trees were planted by the abbot after Liu's earlier banishment. While "Mister Liu" is

The Peach Blossoms of Hsuantu Temple

LIU YU-HSI

Red dust from purple paths swirls before their faces
everyone says they've been to see the flowers
thousands of peach trees at Hsuantu Temple
and all of them planted since Mister Liu departed

clearly a mask for the author, it ostensibly refers to Liu Ch'en, an herb
gatherer who became lost in the Tientai Mountains and survived on
peaches until he finally returned two hundred years later.

115

再遊玄都觀　劉禹錫

百畝庭中半是苔　桃花淨盡菜花開
種桃道士歸何處　前度劉郎今又來

Liu wrote this poem in April of 828 and included this preface: "In the year
805, when I was serving as vice-director of the State Farm Bureau, there
were no flowers at this temple. That was the year I was demoted to serve
as prefect of Lienchou [in Kuangtung province] and later as vice-prefect
of Changte [in Hunan province]. After ten years I was called back to the
capital, and everyone told me there was a Taoist priest who had planted
heavenly peach trees that filled his temple with clouds of red blossoms. So
I wrote the previous poem to record such an unusual sight. Again I was
sent away, and now after fourteen years I have returned once more, this
time to serve as director of the Bureau of Receptions. Once more I visited
Hsuantu Temple, but not a single tree was standing—nothing but useless
weeds swayed in the spring breeze. Therefore, I am writing four more lines
in anticipation of my next outing." The temple courtyard is a reference to

Visiting Hsuantu Temple Again

LIU YU-HSI

The temple's vast courtyard is now home to moss
vegetables flower where peach trees once bloomed
where is the priest who planted the trees
Old Mister Liu is back here again

that of the palace, and the Taoist priest to the former prime minister,
Wang Shu-wen. Again Liu went too far in his sarcastic references. Not long
after writing this poem he was sent off on another "outing."

116

滁州西澗　韋應物

獨憐幽草澗邊生　上有黃鸝深樹鳴
春潮帶雨晚來急　野渡無人舟自橫

Wei Ying-wu (737–792) grew up in Ch'ang-an, where he was recognized as a prodigy and given his first appointment at fifteen as a member of the heir apparent's retinue. After serving in a number of posts in the two capitals, he resigned in 765 and devoted himself to poetry, his family, and his friends. He returned to government service in 781 but was soon rusticated to a series of prefectures near the Yangtze. He wrote this poem in the spring of 785 while serving as prefect of Chuchou, one hundred kilometers west of Nanching. After spending the day wandering through the countryside across the Shangma River (Chuchou's West Stream) west of the city, he returned so late he had to pull himself across on the cable boat kept there for ferrying people back and forth. Commentators are divided over whether this is a simple descriptive poem or whether political implications lie beneath its surface, in which case the neglected plants would refer to virtuous officials and the orioles to those whose voices are heard

Chuchou's West Stream

WEI YING-WU

I love unnoticed plants that grow beside a stream
orioles singing overhead somewhere in a tree
at dusk the current quickens fed by springtime rain
I pull myself across an unmanned country ferry

but ignored. The last couplet recalls similar lines in the *Book of Odes* that
refer to spurned genius. It also suggests that political conditions are wors-
ening, and that there is nothing left to do but save oneself. Then again,
maybe this is just a poem about having the countryside to oneself on a
rainy day.

117

花影　蘇軾

重重疊疊上瑤臺
幾度呼童掃不開
剛被太陽收拾去
卻教明月送將來

Many commentators interpret this poem by Su Shih (1037–1101) as a political critique: the alabaster terrace (which appears in verse 98 as part of the courtyard of the Queen Mother of the West) represents the Sung court, and the flowers represent the reforms of Wang An-shih (1021–1086). In this light, their shadows signify their perceived benefits, the boy stands for the poet or those who listened to his advice, and the sun stands for Emperor Shen-tsung (r. 1068–1085), who supported Wang's reforms. As soon as the emperor died, the reforms were overturned by Empress Dowager Hsuan-jen, who took over as Regent until 1093, when her son was old enough to rule. Unfortunately, Emperor Che-tsung (r. 1086–1100), represented here by the moon, reintroduced the reforms, and Su Shih was once more banished. While such symbolism might well lie beneath the surface, the poem does fine without such baggage.

Flower Shadows

SU SHIH

Layer upon layer on the alabaster terrace
I tell the boy to sweep them up in vain
just as the sun takes them all away
the full moon brings them back again

118

北山　王安石

北山輸綠漲橫陂
直塹回塘灩灩時
細數落花因坐久
緩尋芳草得歸遲

Wang An-shih (1021–1086) grew up in Hangchou and spent most of his career in the Sung capital of Kaifeng, where he rose to the rank of prime minister during the reign of Shen-tsung (r. 1068–1085). In an attempt to relieve the economic plight of farmers, Wang introduced a series of financial reforms that divided the court and that actually increased the hardships of the rural poor due to their irregular implementation. But regardless of what his enemies thought of his politics, everyone agreed Wang was one of the country's greatest poets and essayists. He wrote this poem toward the end of his life, after he had retired to his country estate on North Mountain, just outside Nanching's Unicorn Gate. Nowadays it's called Burnished Gold Mountain (Tzuchinshan) and is better known for the mausoleum where Sun Yat-sen's remains are kept. Looking south, Wang's view included a small crescent-shaped lake next to Pipa Village at the foot of the mountain, the long, narrow moat along the city's east wall,

North Mountain

WANG AN-SHIH

North Mountain sends down green flooding the embankment
the city moat and crescent lake shimmer in the light
counting every falling petal I forget the time
searching for sweet-smelling plants I return home late

and the embankment of the Chinhuai River at the southern edge of the
city. The expression "sweet-smelling plants" (*fang-ts'ao*) also referred to
men of virtue. The phrase was made famous by Ch'u Yuan (340–278 B.C.),
whose insistence on the fragrance of righteousness, as opposed to the
stench of self-interest, resulted in his banishment.

119

湖上　徐元杰

花開紅樹亂鶯啼　草長平湖白鷺飛
風日晴和人意好　夕陽簫鼓幾船歸

Hsu Yuan-chieh (1196–1245) was a native of Shangjao in Kiangsi province. At the Southern Sung capital in Hangchou he was known for his outspoken views, but he still managed to serve as vice-minister in the Court of Imperial Sacrifices and also in the Ministry of Works. Here, he describes Hangchou's West Lake on a fine day in late spring. The lake was created during the previous four centuries by dredging its mud to create several small islands and a series of dikes. When the Sung dynasty transferred its capital to Hangchou, the city's new lake soon became the talk of the country. And despite its relatively small size—four square miles—it has remained the most famous lake in China.

On the Lake

HSU YUAN-CHIEH

Orioles chatter madly in trees of red blossoms
egrets converge on a lake of tall grass
everyone loves a clear mild day
boats return at dusk on waves of flutes and drums

120

漫興　杜甫

糝徑楊花鋪白氈　點溪荷葉疊青錢

筍根稚子無人見　沙上鳧雛傍母眠

This was the seventh of a series of nine poems Tu Fu (712–770) wrote in 761 when he was living just outside the provincial capital of Chengtu. The fifth poem in this series is verse 112. Here, he describes the simple yet remarkable scene around his cottage as spring gives way to summer.

Inspired

TU FU

Willow fuzz lines the path with bolts of white felt
lily pads dot the stream with stacks of green coins
the offspring of bamboo haven't yet appeared
ducklings on the shore sleep beside their mother

121

春晴　王駕

雨前初見花間蕊　雨後全無葉底花
蜂蝶紛紛過牆去　卻疑春色在鄰家

Wang Chia (b. 851) has left little information about himself other than that he was from Yungchi at the southwest corner of Shansi province and that he served as prefect of several outlying districts as well as vice-director of one of the bureaus in the Ministry of Rites. Although this poem ostensibly describes the poet's garden, many critics read it as a commentary on the fickleness of human sentiment: the center of attention one day, without friends the next. Even when they enjoyed the emperor's support, the only thing of which officials were certain is that it wouldn't last. But the only alternatives for someone educated in the Confucian classics and literary models was to teach in the village school, to serve as someone's secretary, or to farm a poor patch of ground—hence the popularity of the hermit tradition in China. Two hundred years after this poem was written, Wang An-shih (1021–1086) took such a liking to it he rewrote it and included it in his own collection.

Spring Clearing

WANG CHIA

Before the rain there were buds among the flowers
when it cleared even those below the leaves were gone
all the bees and butterflies flew across the wall
apparently spring has moved to the neighbor's

122

春暮　曹豳

門外無人問落花　綠陰冉冉遍天涯
林鶯啼到無聲處　青草池塘獨聽蛙

Ts'ao Pin (1170–1249) was from Wenchou in Chekiang and served in a number of posts, including judicial commissioner of his home province, rectifier of omissions, and member of the Hanlin Academy. Apparently he, too, suffered the loss of imperial favor. While the poet sighs at the transience of spring, he also voices a complaint about the replacement of the melodious orioles at court with the croaking of lesser talents.

Late Spring

TS'AO PIN

No one comes out to look at fallen flowers
a canopy of green slowly veils the sky
the orioles in the trees have finally stopped singing
I only hear frogs in the grass-filled pond

落花　朱淑貞

連理枝頭花正開　妒花風雨便相摧
願教青帝常為主　莫遣紛紛點翠苔

Chu Shu-chen (d. 1233) grew up in Hangchou in a well-off family and became adept at poetry and painting as a young girl. However, her education far outstripped the needs of her social position, and she spent most of her life in Suchou as the wife of a minor official who was often away on extended assignments and with whom she had little in common. Instead of sewing, she wrote poems and became known throughout the country for her plaintive verses on a woman's unequal place in Chinese society. In fact, during the Southern Sung dynasty her poetry was better known than that of her fellow woman poet Li Ch'ing-chiao (1084–1155). When she died, Chu's parents burned most of what she had written as an offering to her departed spirit. Still, many of her poems were so well known they survived, in an edition published several decades after her death. The intertwined branches represent the union of lovers, while the King of Green (Ch'ing Ti) is the god of spring.

Falling Flowers

CHU SHU-CHEN

Whenever intertwined branches bloom
the jealous wind and rain strip away their flowers
if only the King of Green could perpetuate his rule
they wouldn't end up scattered across the moss

124

開一
到從春
荼梅暮
蘼粉遊
花褪小
事殘園
了粧
　　王
絲塗淇
絲抹
天新
棘紅
出上
莓海
牆棠

Wang Ch'i (Sung dynasty) has left no information about himself other than what can be derived from a few poems. Here, he provides us with the sequence of attention in this small garden, which is probably somewhere south of the Yangtze, perhaps in the Southern Sung capital of Hangchou. It was during this period that the plum came to symbolize Chinese resistance to Khitan aggression and the loss of North China, and it was planted extensively in the Hangchou area. See, for example, Sung Po-jen's *Guide to Capturing a Plum Blossom*. As plum blossoms fall in early spring they are replaced in this garden by the ruby-tipped flowers of the begonia, which are joined by the white, grandiflora blooms of the Chinese raspberry, or *Rubus rosifolius* var. *commersonii*, both of which then give way to summer greenery. The name *t'ien-chi* (some editions have *yao* for *t'ien*, apparently a copyist error) sometimes referred to the Chinese asparagus vine, but here it refers to the willow.

Visiting a Private Garden in Late Spring

WANG CH'I

Once the plum casts off its faded charms
fresh rouge graces the begonia
which lasts until raspberry petals are gone
and willow catkins hang across the mossy wall

125

鶯梭　劉克莊

擲柳遷喬太有情　交交時作弄機聲
洛陽三月花如錦　多少功夫織得成

Liu K'o-chuang (1187–1269) was from Putien in Fukien province and was one of the leading literary critics of his time. He was also its most prolific writer and was considered the most important poet of the Rivers and Lakes school of poetry. Although he served in important posts in the Ministry of Works and the Central Secretariat, he became disgusted by court politics and spent his final decade living in simple circumstances in the countryside. Liu was reportedly the original compiler of this anthology—though his arrangement was topical rather than based on formal and seasonal categories, and this poem must have been added by a later compiler in honor of Liu's earlier efforts. The images of the first line are indebted to the poem "Cutting Wood" in the Hsiaoya section of the *Book of Odes*: "They come from dark valleys / they settle among treetops / twittering they call / in search of a friend."

The Oriole Shuttle

LIU K'O-CHUANG

Through the willows to the treetops so full of feeling
twittering on the wing they sound like a loom
Loyang in April is a tapestry of flowers
but it takes so much effort to weave

126

暮春即事　葉采

雙雙瓦雀行書案　點點楊花入硯池
閒坐小窗讀周易　不知春去幾多時

Yeh Ts'ai (c. 1190–1240) was a native of Shaowu in Fukien province. Although he was a famous Confucian scholar of his day and director of the Palace Library in Hangchou, he makes fun here of his own immersion in the philosophy of change and his failure to pay attention to the changes taking place in the world around him. The *Yiching* (*Book of Changes*) was the primary text used by neo-Confucians during the Sung dynasty for developing something comparable to Taoist cosmology and Buddhist psychology. The book dates back to the beginning of the Chou dynasty, or 1100 B.C., and divides the dynamic forces in the world into sixty-four modes, each represented by a series of six lines and explained by a written commentary. But the sight of swallows busy building their nests, and willow fuzz in his inkwell, suddenly brings Yeh back to the mundane world. During the Sung the Chinese still sat on floor mats, and scholars used a small table or bookrest about one foot high for their texts and writing

Events of Late Spring

House swallows swoop in pairs above my desk
willow fuzz floats in my inkwell
below my small window reading the *Book of Changes*
I wonder how long spring has been over

materials. The Chinese version of the inkwell consisted in a depression at
one end of a slate slab, where ink accumulated once it was ground with
drops of water on the slab's surface. The small window suggests poverty.
Often the mouth of a broken pottery container was used for the frame. It
also suggests the narrow-minded focus on studies characteristic of those
preparing for the civil service exams.

127

登山　李涉

終日昏昏醉夢間　忽聞春盡強登山
因過竹院逢僧話　又得浮生半日閒

Li She (fl. 830) was the son of a prominent Loyang family, but he preferred a simpler, unfettered life. When he was still a young man he and his younger brother, Li Po, lived as recluses on Lushan, overlooking the Yangtze. Later, he was recommended to the court and served briefly in Ch'ang-an as an advisor to the crown prince. But he did not get along with those in power and was banished, called back, and then banished again. When he wrote this poem he was serving not far downriver from Nanching in Chenchiang. In the *Chuantangshih* this poem is entitled "Written at the Monks' Quarters of Holin Temple." This temple was located on Yellow Crane Mountain outside Chenchiang's South Gate, beyond the estates of the town's well-to-do. Two hundred years later, one of China's greatest calligraphers, Mi Fei, became so fond of this temple that he asked to be buried by its front gate. The temple is gone but Mi Fei's grave is still there.

Climbing a Mountain

LI SHE

All day I feel lost as if drunk or in a dream
then I hear spring is over and force myself to climb
passing a bamboo courtyard I meet a monk and talk
and spend another afternoon beyond this floating life

128

蠶婦吟　謝枋得

子規啼徹四更時　起視蠶稠怕葉稀
不信樓頭楊柳月　玉人歌舞未曾歸

Hsieh Fang-te (1226–1289) was from Yiyang in Kiangsi province. Prior to his imprisonment in Beijing he served in several posts in the Southern Sung capital of Hangchou, which is still famous for its silk brocade. During this period, taxes were paid in lengths of silk, and each household had a quota to meet and someone assigned to fill it. To the Chinese, the cuckoo's cry sounds like the phrase *pu-ju kuei-ch'u* ("better go home"), and during spring it often cries all night. In an effort to guard against thieves and fires, Chinese in urban areas divided the night into five two-hour watches. Here, the servant in charge of the household silk quota has been kept awake by the cuckoo's cry and gets up after midnight to feed the silkworms, which were kept on wicker trays in a warm part of the house and fed a diet of mulberry leaves until they spun themselves into their cocoons. But not only does this silkmaid have a hard life, so does her mistress, who has to stay up all night entertaining others. This poem, as with

Lament of the Silkmaid

HSIEH FANG-TE

Until the fourth watch the cuckoo cries
she gets up to see if the silkworms have leaves
surprised at the moon between rooftops and willows
and her mistress not back from the party

verse 113, was not part of Liu K'o-chuang's original anthology and was
probably added to include something from one of the major writers of the
Sung dynasty's final years.

129

晚春　韓愈

草木知春不久歸　百般紅紫鬥芳菲
楊花榆莢無才思　惟解漫天作雪飛

Han Yu (768–824) was born into a family of scholars in Menghsien in Honan province. Orphaned at the age of two, he grew up in the family of his elder brother, under whose guidance he received his early education while moving from post to post in the provinces. After finally passing the civil service exam he enjoyed success in the central government — where he eventually rose to the rank of chief minister of the Secretariat — and also in the literary realm, where he was admired as one of the dynasty's greatest poets and essayists. Han was an ardent follower of Confucian tradition but was adept at adapting it to the times. In his poetry he strove to be clear and concise, and he often used the language of ordinary speech to this end. Here, he portrays a scene in late spring, which many commentators read as a comparison of ostentatious sycophants to simpler officials who have no other means of gaining the court's attention than through their pure-hearted virtue.

Late Spring

HAN YU

Every plant and tree knows spring will soon be gone
a hundred pinks and purples compete with their bouquets
willow fuzz and elm pods lack such clever means
they only know how to fill the sky with snow

130

傷春　楊萬里

準擬今春樂事濃　依然枉卻一東風
年年不帶看花眼　不是愁中即病中

Yang Wan-li (1124–1206) was from Chishui in Kiangsi province. He was so devoted to literature, it was said, that he favored a good poem over a beautiful woman. Despite such devotion, or perhaps because of it, he managed to become a member of the Institute of Academicians and, eventually, director of the Palace Library. However, his frequent disagreements with official policy resulted in a career spent mostly in the provinces. In 1178, while serving on the Grand Canal as prefect of Changchou, he came to a new understanding of poetic technique. Breaking with the more formal style favored by members of the ruling elite, Yang created poems that were known for their clarity and humor and their use of everyday speech. He retired to his hometown in 1192, and by the time of his death he was considered one of the greatest poets of the Southern Sung. In the *Sungshih-chiao* this poem is entitled "Hiking Up Wanhua Valley at Dawn to See Begonias." The East Wind rises with the sun as it returns from its annual southerly migration in spring.

Spring Lament

YANG WAN-LI

I was hoping joy would overflow this spring
as usual I've wasted another East Wind
it's been years since I could look at flowers
if not because of cares then illness

131

送春　王逢原

三月殘花落更開　小簷日日燕飛來
子規夜半猶啼血　不信東風喚不回

Wang Feng-yuan (1032–1059), aka Wang Ling, was a native of Yangchou, where the Grand Canal meets the Yangtze. Although he was quite poor he was such a brilliant student that he came to the attention of Wang An-shih, before he became prime minister. Wang An-shih admired his talents and virtue so much he considered him an equal and arranged for him to marry his wife's younger sister. Unfortunately, Wang Feng-yuan did not live long enough to realize his potential: he died of an illness before he was thirty. The swallow is the bird most commonly associated with summer, while the oriole and cuckoo are the birds of early and late spring. The East Wind is the wind of spring, just as the West Wind is the wind of autumn.

Seeing Off Spring

WANG FENG-YUAN

In April flowers fade and fall and more appear
swallows fly below the eaves back and forth all day
the cuckoo cries at midnight as if its voice would break
convinced it can still call the East Wind back

132

三月晦日送春　賈島

三月正當三十日　風光別我苦吟身
共君今夜不須睡　未到曉鐘猶是春

Chia Tao (779–843) was a native of the Beijing area but moved to Loyang and later Ch'ang-an as a young man. At first he chose the life of a monk but then changed his mind and decided he would rather devote his life to poetry. Although he failed to attain even minor distinction as an official, he became well known for his plaintive, well-crafted verses, some of which took years to write, and his poetry greatly influenced later generations of poets. Han Yu (768–824), who was a major influence on him, once wrote, "When Meng Chiao [751–814] died and was buried at Peimang [the grave-yard outside Loyang] / the sun moon and stars suddenly felt bored / worried that literature had come to an end / Heaven gave the world Chia Tao." The dawn bell is that of a monastery, which will soon rouse Chia Tao's former colleagues in their quest to transcend their own attachments. In some editions this poem is entitled "For Judge Liu on the Last Day of April." In the Chinese calendar April (the third lunar month) is the last month of spring.

274

Seeing Off Spring on the Last Day of April

CHIA TAO

When April reaches its thirtieth day
your wind and light forsake a poor poet
I don't want to sleep with you tonight
until the dawn bell you're still spring

133

客中初夏　司馬光

四月清和雨乍晴　南山當戶轉分明
更無柳絮因風起　惟有葵花向日傾

Ssu-ma Kuang (1019–1086) was born in Hsiahsien in Shansi province and grew up in Loyang. In the course of a distinguished career at the Sung capital in Kaifeng, he led the political faction that opposed the financial reforms of Wang An-shih. Not long after Shen-tsung (r. 1068–1085) ascended the throne, Ssu-ma Kuang was demoted and sent to what was once Ch'ang-an, where he wrote this poem. He was allowed to return to his home in Loyang the following year (1071) on the condition that he avoid politics, which he did until the young Che-tsung ascended the throne in 1086 and made him prime minister. Ssu-ma Kuang died later that same year. Here, he looks out his door during the summer he spent in Ch'ang-an and remarks on the seasonal changes that remind him of life at court. These mountains south of Ch'ang-an were a common metaphor for imperial and dynastic long life, while the willow fuzz of late spring represents officials who float on any passing breeze, and the sunflowers of early summer

Away from Home at the Beginning of Summer

SSU-MA KUANG

In May when it's mild and the rain finally stops
the Chungnan Mountains appear in my door
willow fuzz no longer swirls in the wind
everywhere sunflowers lean toward the sun

stand for loyal officials such as the poet himself. According to this analogy
the summer sun would be the newly crowned emperor, Shen-tsung, for
whom Ssu-ma Kuang has not yet given up hope.

134

有約　趙師秀

黃梅時節家家雨
青草池塘處處蛙
有約不來過夜半
閒敲棋子落燈花

Chao Shih-hsiu (d. 1219) was a native of Yungchia in southern Chekiang province and was one of the founders of what became known as the Rivers and Lakes school of poetry, which championed the works of such poets as Chia Tao and the subjects of everyday life, and which opposed the use of refined language and courtly themes favored by the Kiangsi school. The Chinese still call this period (when early summer rains coincide with the ripening of plums) *mei-yu* (plum rains), which keeps everyone but farmers indoors and keeps friends away. The game of *wei-ch'i* (Japanese: *go*) originated in China more than three thousand years ago: it involves the placement of small black and white stones on a chessboard of inter-secting lines, with the object being the occupation of territory and removal of the opponent's pieces.

Waiting for a Friend

CHAO SHIH-HSIU

During plum season it rains on every roof
around the grassy pond frogs are everywhere
waiting after midnight for a friend who doesn't come
I play a game of chess until the lamp goes out

135

初夏睡起　楊萬里

梅子留酸濺齒牙
芭蕉分綠上窗紗
日長睡起無情思
閒看兒童捉柳花

When Yang Wan-li (1124–1206) was serving as prefect of Changchou, he experienced a kind of enlightenment he equated with that of Zen and began writing in a simple, spontaneous style. Eventually he produced over 20,000 poems, some 4,000 of which survive. Here, he has been taking a midday nap and quenches his thirst with some plums. Gazing outside his windows, screened with silk the density of cheesecloth to keep out insects in summer, he watches his children chase willow fuzz, which is itself a sign that spring is over. Such are the pleasures of early summer for those who don't chase fame or fortune.

Waking Up in Early Summer

YANG WAN-LI

The sour trace of plums squirts between my teeth
the light green of bananas fills my window screen
waking up at noon without a thought or care
I sit and watch my children chasing willow fuzz

136

三衢道中　曾幾

梅子黃時日日晴　小溪汎盡卻山行

綠陰不減來時路　添得黃鸝四五聲

Tseng Chi (1084–1166) was born in Kanchou near the southern border of Kiangsi province and grew up in Loyang. He is better known to history as the teacher of the Sung-dynasty lyric poet Lu Yu (1125–1210), but during his career he served as judicial commissioner of Kiangsi and Chekiang and eventually headed the Ministry of Rites and the Secretariat. At one point he was forced into temporary retirement when Ch'in Kuei was prime minister, but he returned upon Ch'in's death. On this occasion he is leaving the Southern Sung capital of Hangchou to take up his new post as prefect of Chuchou at the southwest corner of Chekiang province, which most officials would have viewed as a demotion. Normally, as noted in verse 134, this season is marked by constant light rains. But this is a poem about finding good fortune where one doesn't expect it — the silver lining in rustication to Chuchou. Taking advantage of good weather, Tseng travels from Hangchou by boat up the Fuchun and Chuchiang Rivers as far as he

On the Sanchu Road

TSENG CHI

Plums are yellow and days are sunny
where the river turns shallow I take the trail
the canopy of green doesn't get less shady
the occasional sound of orioles though is new

can go and then continues on foot over Sanchu Mountain for the final
part of the journey. As he nears his destination he hears the welcome
songs of like-minded poets.

137

即景　朱淑貞

竹搖清影罩幽窗　兩兩時禽噪夕陽
謝卻海棠飛盡絮　困人天氣日初長

Chu Shu-chen (fl. 1200) grew up in Hangchou in a family that produced a number of officials. Her uncle was the great neo-Confucian philosopher Chu Hsi (1130–1200). She was somewhat of a prodigy herself as a young girl, and as a result of her family background she received an unusually good education. After she married she moved to Suchou. But her marriage was not a happy one and her husband was often away. She was also a skilled musician and calligrapher, but her fame rested on her poems, especially those employing the voice of the abandoned woman. The houses of the rich included a series of courtyards, and the place where the wife lived would have been in the back, hidden from the view of visitors. The pairs of birds remind Chu of her own isolation, and the disappearance of the signs of spring of her own fading beauty. This part of China, near the Yangtze Delta, is known for its hot, humid summers.

Impressions

CHU SHU-CHEN

Swaying bamboo shadows shade my secluded window
summer birds chatter in pairs in the sunset
begonias have faded and willow fuzz has flown
the enervating days are starting to get longer

138

初夏游張園　戴敏

乳鴨池塘水淺深　熟梅天氣半晴陰
東園載酒西園醉　摘盡枇杷一樹金

Tai Min (fl. 1170) was a native of Huangyen in Chekiang province and the father of Tai Fu-ku, who was a prominent poet of the Rivers and Lakes school of poetry. Neither the father nor the son (to whom some editions attribute this poem) served in the government. Here, the poet spends a day following the sun across a friend's garden—from the eastern half that greets the sun to the western half that sees it off. The loquat looks similar to a small apricot and ripens in early summer, about the same time as the plum. Both are often enjoyed with rice wine or stronger spirits. It was during the Sung dynasty that garden landscape became a major art form, especially in such cities as Suchou and Hangchou. One mainland Chinese commentator complains that there is no social value in a poem such as this. Indeed, one cannot put a price on it.

Visiting Chang's Garden at the Beginning of Summer

TAI MIN

Ducklings in a pond of deep and shallow water
plum-season weather partly clear and cloudy
taking wine to the East Garden we get drunk in the West
beneath a loquat tree picked clean of gold

139

鄂州南樓書事　黃庭堅

四顧山光接水光　憑欄十里芰荷香

清風明月無人管　並作南來一味涼

Huang T'ing-chien (1045–1105) was from Hsiushui in Kiangsi province and was ranked with his mentor, Su Shih (1037–1101), as one of the great calligraphers and poets of the Sung. He was also the founder of the Kiangsi school of poetry and was known for his layered allusions and irregular rhythms. Although some critics consider him too careful in his poetic constructions, and others judge his poetry superficial, he responds here to a poem by Su Shih with a masterful treatment of the simplest of scenes. During his banishment in 1080 to Huangchou, just downriver from Wu-chang (Ochou), Su wrote his famous "Red Cliff Ode," which includes the lines: "the cool breeze on the river / the bright moon above the mountains / the ear turns things into sounds / the eye turns things into sights / the endless treasury of these creators / you and I enjoy together." Huang also suffered several banishments. On this occasion he was being rusticated farther up the Yangtze to serve as prefect of Chiangling. Stopping in

Written at the South Tower of Ochou

HUANG T'ING-CHIEN

Mountain light meets water light everywhere I look
from the railing I can smell miles of water lilies
the soft wind and bright moon aren't controlled by man
together from the south they bring something cool

Wuchang, he wrote this poem while looking out onto the lily-covered
expanse of the city's South Lake. Political overtones rise to the surface at
the end, where the poet turns his back on the human politics of the north-
ern capital. The South Wind became a common metaphor for benevolent
government after Emperor Shun (r. 2300 B.C.) composed the lines: "The
touch of the South Wind can relieve my people's pains." Also, while the
sun's ecliptic moves north during the summer, the path of the full moon
moves south. Some editions wrongly attribute this poem to Wang An-shih.

140

山亭夏日　高駢

綠樹陰濃夏日長　樓臺倒影入池塘
水晶簾動微風起　滿架薔薇一院香

Kao P'ien (821–887) was from Beijing. After serving in senior military posts along China's northern, western, and southern frontiers, he was appointed military commissioner of the Huainan section of the Yangtze in 879 and successfully defended the key city of Yangchou against the rebel forces of Huang Ch'ao. However, he also intentionally avoided attacking the rebels in favor of protecting his own position, thus ensuring the end of the T'ang dynasty. Kao later died at the hands of Pi Shih-to, another bandit leader. Here, he anticipates the end of the dynasty, which is represented by the upside-down pavilion, and the beginning of a new dynasty, which is suggested by the moving curtain and rising breeze. The prickly rose, or *Rosa acicularis*, is known for its perfume. Here, its scented flowers refer to men of greater virtue than those who filled the court when this poem was written. No doubt Kao had in mind his friends and associates in the Yangchou area.

A Mountain Pavilion on a Summer Day

KAO P'IEN

The shade from trees is dense and summer days are long
an upside-down pavilion is mirrored in the pond
crystal curtains shimmer in the faintest wind
a trellis of roses fills the courtyard with perfume

141

畫出耕田夜績麻　村莊兒女各當家
童孫未解供耕織　也傍桑陰學種瓜

田家　范成大

Fan Ch'eng-ta (1126–1193) was from Suchou in Kiangsu province. He served in a number of posts but is chiefly remembered for his staunch re-fusal, while serving as ambassador to the Chin Tartars in North China, to betray national interests even when threatened with death. He was also ranked as one of the four greatest poets of the Southern Sung dynasty and was known for his objective, realistic style and his focus on the everyday events of farm life. Eventually, court politics became too much for him, and in 1183 he retired to the countryside just outside Suchou. This is one in a series of sixty poems he wrote not long afterwards entitled "Occa-sional Poems on the Four Seasons of Farm Life," a series that served as the model for many later poets. The mulberry trees produced the leaves that fed the silkworms that made the silk that paid the taxes that supported the imperial lifestyle.

A Farm Family

FAN CH'ENG-TA

Weeding fields at sunup twisting hemp at night
village boys and girls all have their chores
even little children too small to plow or weave
learn to plant melons in the shade of mulberry trees

142

鄉綠　村
村遍　莊
四山　即
月原　事
閒白
人滿　范
少川　成
　　　大
縵子
了規
蠶聲
桑裏
又雨
插如
田煙

Some editions attribute this poem to Weng Chuan (fl. 1250), one of the Four Poet Laureates of Yungchia. The white water here is the result of the "plum rains" that fall in May and June (the fourth lunar month) in Central and Southern China. During this time of year the cuckoo's cry, which normally sounds like *pu-ju kuei-ch'u* ("better go home"), sounds like *k'uai k'uai ch'a-ho* ("hurry up and plant rice"). About the same time that silkworms wake from their winter slumber, farmers transplant rice sprouts from seedlings started a month or more earlier.

Village Events

FAN CH'ENG-TA

Green covers hills and plains and white fills the rivers
in the cuckoo's cry there's a misty rain
idle folks are rare the Fourth Month in a village
once silkworms are fed it's time to transplant rice

143

題榴花　朱熹

五月榴花照眼明　枝間時見子初成
可憐此地無車馬　顛倒蒼苔落絳英

Chu Hsi (1130–1200) was born in Fukien province but made his home in Anhui. He enjoyed a relatively successful career in the government, but he was far better known as one of the leading proponents of neo-Confucianism, which dominated intellectual life during the Sung dynasty. In fact, ever since the Sung, every student's education in the Confucian classics has begun with Chu Hsi's commentaries. The pomegranate arrived in China from Central Asia via the Silk Road more than a thousand years before this poem was written. But within a few hundred years of its arrival it became so popular that people started calling the fifth lunar month Pomegranate Month. This is when its red fruit begins to form, while the flower is still in bloom. The fruit itself often appears in Chinese art as a symbol for a womb that contains countless offspring. The poet is also reminded that, like the pomegranate, his own neo-Confucian ideas are full

On the Pomegranate Flower

CHU HSI

> Pomegranate flowers brighten eyes in June
> as soon as they appear their fruit begins to form
> but neither carts nor horses visit this poor place
> where ruby blossoms lie upon the emerald moss

of promise, and yet the country's elite (on horseback or in horse-drawn carts) do not pay them the attention they deserve. Some editions attribute this poem to Han Yu (768–824).

144

村晚　雷震

草滿池塘水滿陂
山銜落日浸寒漪
牧童歸去橫牛背
短笛無腔信口吹

Lei Chen (*lei* means "thunder" and *chen* means "shake") lived during the Sung dynasty, but nothing else is known about him—which is surprising, as commentators marvel at the combination of effortlessness and craftsmanship in this poem. Perhaps he was a friend of the compiler and preferred anonymity. Among the duties assigned children in farming communities was the tending of oxen (in North China) or water buffaloes (in the South). The back of the water buffalo, though, is much broader and provides a better seat. The transverse flute arrived in China in prehistoric times and apparently originated with one of the nomadic groups along the country's northwest border, where eagle bones were used before the Chinese replaced them with bamboo.

Village Dusk

LEI CHEN

Grass lines the pond and water lines the bank
the sun sinks in the mountains and in the icy ripples
a herdboy returns on the back of his ox
aimlessly blowing a flute to no tune

145

書湖陰先生壁　王安石

茅簷常掃淨無苔　花木成蹊手自栽
一水護田將綠遶　兩山排闥送青來

Wang An-shih (1021–1086) was the most controversial political figure of the Sung dynasty, as well as one of its greatest calligraphers, writers, and poets. He wrote this near the end of his life, while living in retirement outside Nanching at the foot of Tzuchinshan. Political undertones seem to have finally disappeared from his verse as he writes a poem to his neighbor, Yang Te-feng, whose pen name was Mister Lakeshade (Hu-yin Hsien-sheng). Sweeping the path before one's house was normally done when expecting a visitor — in this case, the poet. This was the first of two poems.

Written on Mister Lakeshade's Wall

WANG AN-SHIH

Below your thatched eaves you've swept away the moss
you yourself planted the path of flowering trees
a stream guards your fields encircling it with green
two peaks swing open and welcome the blue

146

朱雀橋邊野草花
烏衣巷口夕陽斜
舊時王謝堂前燕
飛入尋常百姓家

烏衣巷　劉禹錫

Liu Yu-hsi (772–842) was from the Grand Canal town of Hsuchou in Kiangsu province. He rose to the position of censor at court but was banished for siding with a group of reformers opposed to the power of the eunuchs, the military, and the aristocracy. This poem is directed against the latter group, though it is conveniently set in the past to avoid political repercussions. In 826 Liu was sent south to serve as prefect of Hohsien. This was one of five poems he wrote while visiting Nanching, not far downriver from his post. During the Six Dynasties (222–589), Red Bird Bridge spanned the Chinhuai River just outside Nanching's South Gate, and Black Robe Lane was just inside the gate. During the Wu dynasty (222–277) this was the location of Black Robe Palace, named for the black-robed officials who hovered around the court. During the subsequent Chin dynasty (278–419) this was where the powerful Wang and Hsieh clans lived. It was also the location of Laiyentang (Arriving Swallow Hall),

Black Robe Lane

LIU YU-HSI

Wildflowers bloom by Red Bird Bridge
the fading light slants down Black Robe Lane
where swallows once lived among Hsiehs and Wangs
they now frequent homes of ordinary people

where they welcomed visiting relatives. Both of these clans were wiped out
at the beginning of the T'ang (618–906). Here, black-robed swallows re-
place the officials.

147

送元二使安西　王維

渭城朝雨浥輕塵　客舍青青柳色新
勸君更盡一杯酒　西出陽關無故人

Wang Wei (701–761) was born in Taiyuan in northern Shansi but grew up in Yungchi at the southern end of the same province. Although he rose to the post of deputy prime minister, he also suffered several banishments. Here, he sees off a friend who was banished to Anhsi, the westernmost part of the Silk Road under Chinese control. As the Silk Road left the Tunhuang oasis it divided into a northern and a southern route, both of which skirted the Taklamakan Desert. Jade Pass marked the beginning of the northern route through Hami and Turfan to Kuche, where the main garrison of the Anhsi Protectorate was located. Yang Pass was twenty kilometers to the south and marked the beginning of the southern route to Khotan and Kashgar. Weicheng (Wei City) was just west of Ch'ang-an on the north shore of the Wei River, near the former Ch'in dynasty (221–207 B.C.) capital of Hsienyang. This was where people held going-away parties for friends heading west—hence the dust. The Chinese word for willow is

Seeing Off Yuan Er on a Mission to Anhsi

WANG WEI

Morning rain dampens the dust in Weicheng
new willow catkins turn an inn green
drink one more cup of wine my friend
west of Yang Pass there's no one you know

a homophone of another word meaning "stay behind." Thus, the Chinese broke off willow catkins to give to friends as a parting memento. The custom apparently began in Ch'ang-an, where the willow's new catkins appeared about the same time that snow melted in the passes. This poem was later set to music and called "The Song of Weicheng." According to Su Shih, the first line was sung once and the last three lines three times.

148

黃鶴樓聞笛　李白

一為遷客去長沙　西望長安不見家
黃鶴樓中聞玉笛　江城五月落梅花

Li Pai (701–762) wrote this poem in 758 when he stopped to visit Wuchang's Yellow Crane Tower after being released from prison for his involvement in the revolt of the emperor's brother. In some editions this poem is titled "Written on the North Gazebo Stele." On one of the tower's stories were four gazebos from which to view the four directions. The north gazebo faced the place where the Han River joins the Yangtze from the west. Li Pai is on his way south to Changsha, the provincial capital of Hunan, and looks back up the Han toward Ch'ang-an. This tower was built in A.D. 223, shortly after the end of the Han dynasty, in honor of the Taoist immortal Fei Wen-wei, who rode off from here on a yellow crane and who sometimes returned to play his jade flute. "Plum Blossoms Fall" was the name of a tune for the flute. The plum is said to transcend winter's adversity and normally blooms during New Year. In the background

On Yellow Crane Tower Hearing a Flute

LI PAI

Suddenly an exile on the way to Changsha
looking back toward Ch'ang-an I don't see a soul
from Yellow Crane Tower I hear a jade flute
plum blossoms fall in this city in June

of this poem is the Han-dynasty poet Chia Yi (200–168 B.C.), who was
unjustly banished to Changsha for his frank and unwelcome advice and
with whom Li Pai clearly identifies.

149

題淮南寺　程顥

南去北來休便休　白蘋吹盡楚江秋
道人不是悲秋客　一任晚山相對愁

Ch'eng Hao (1032–1085) was from Loyang. He and his younger brother, Ch'eng Yi (1033–1107), were among the earliest and most eloquent spokesmen for the Sung dynasty's neo-Confucian philosophy, which incorporated elements of Taoism and Buddhism. Here, the older brother demonstrates the detachment of such understanding, as he stops at a Taoist temple just outside Yangchou where the Grand Canal meets the Yangtze. Arriving too late to cross the river, he watches the sun setting on the hills along both shores and notices that the floating duckweed, whose white blooms line the Yangtze in early autumn, has already finished flowering. Duckweed also represents the poet's own rootless existence as an official, subject to imperial whim or displeasure. The region along both shores of the Yangtze was controlled at one time or another by the ancient state of Ch'u, one of its famous poets being Sung Yu (290–223 B.C.), who began his "Nine Arguments" with the line: "How mournful the season of autumn."

Written at Huainan Temple

CH'ENG HAO

Traveling north heading south stopping where they can
duckweed blooms depart Ch'u waterways by fall
a man of the Way doesn't mourn autumn
let the evening hills share each other's sorrow

150

七夕　楊朴

未會牽牛意若何　須邀織女弄金梭

年年乞與人間巧　不道人間巧幾多

Yang P'u (921–1003) was from Chengchou in Honan province and spent a good deal of his life in the countryside near the Yellow River, where he was known for riding everywhere on his ox. Trying to avoid the conflicts of the Five Dynasties Period (907–960), he lived as a recluse for several years on Sungshan. But he was finally called out of seclusion at the beginning of the Sung dynasty, and he served briefly as an official in the capital of Kaifeng. According to an ancient Chinese folktale, the Emperor of Heaven had a daughter who wove heavenly cloth with her golden loom. Realizing she was lonely, he arranged for her to marry a herdboy. But after they were married she forgot all about weaving. This made the emperor so angry he banished the lovers to different shores of the Milky Way and only allowed them to meet one night a year, on the seventh night of the seventh lunar month. But instead of making love this night, the Herdboy asks his wife to show the world how to weave celestial cloth. Until modern times,

The Seventh Night

YANG P'U

I've never understood the Herdboy's thoughts
why he asks the Weaving Maid to work her golden loom
every year offering her skill to the world
unaware the world has enough skills already

it was customary for women to make offerings to the Weaving Maid on
this night in exchange for her blessings on their own handiwork. In con-
trasting the simple generosity of the celestial couple with the wily ways of
the world, the poet reflects his own view of the times in which he lived.

151

秋　朱熹
月

清溪流過碧山頭　空水澄鮮一色秋
隔斷紅塵三十里　白雲紅葉兩悠悠

Chu Hsi (1130–1200) wrote this poem around 1180 while traveling through the mountains to Kao-an, southwest of the capital of Kiangsi province. Chu Hsi was serving as governor at the time. The neo-Confucian point of view is as clear as the moonlight in this poem. Everything is part of everything else, and yet everything has its own nature. Red dust (*hung-ch'en*) was a term used by Chinese Buddhists when referring to the world of sensation. Some editions attribute this poem to Ch'eng Hao.

Autumn Moon

CHU HSI

A pure stream flows past a jade green peak
the water and the sky have the clear look of fall
dozens of miles from the world of red dust
white clouds and yellow leaves appear without end

152

立秋　劉翰

乳鴉啼散玉屏空
睡起秋聲無覓處

一枕新涼一扇風
滿階梧葉月明中

Liu Han (fl. 1190), aka Liu Wu-tzu, was from Changsha in Hunan province, but little else is known about him. In addition to their calendar of twelve lunar months, the Chinese also divide the year into twenty-four solar periods. Autumn at the Gate (*Li-ch'iu*) occurs at the end of the first week of August. Most commentators are convinced the jade screen here refers to an elegant, jade-colored silk or paper screen—as it does in the next poem. But why would anyone put up a screen to block the wind at this time of year, when the first cool breeze of autumn is so welcome? It makes more sense to read it as a metaphor for a cloudless (and duckless) sky. Paulownias are planted for their shade. Their huge leaves are a foot or two across, and when they fall at the beginning of autumn, they all fall at once.

Autumn at the Gate

LIU HAN

The quacking is gone the jade screen is empty
my pillow feels cool fanned by the wind
autumn sounds wake me but where are their traces
paulownia leaves cover the steps in the moonlight

銀燭秋光冷畫屏

輕羅小扇撲流螢

天街夜色涼如水

臥看牽牛織女星

秋夕

杜牧

Tu Mu (803–852) was born in Ch'ang-an to a family that had lost its wealth and power by the time he was a boy. Although he began his studies late, he excelled in the literary arts and served in a number of posts, though of ever-decreasing importance. Here, he expresses his disappointment through the persona of one of the emperor's concubines. With the passing of summer, her fan has lost its function, and her ability to affect her own life is reduced to trying to swat fireflies. The "streets of Heaven" refers to those in the forbidden precincts where only the Son of Heaven and his concubines and eunuch attendants lived. During the hours after sunset on the seventh night of the seventh lunar month, the Weaving Maid and Herdboy stars (Vega and Altair) are directly overhead on either side of the Milky Way. And though they only meet one night a year on a bridge formed by the wings of magpies, this is still more frequent than this woman's rendezvous with the emperor. Likewise, Tu Mu, who was

Autumn Evening

TU MU

Silver lantern autumn light chills her painted screen
she swats at passing fireflies with her small silk fan
at night the streets of Heaven look as cool as water
lying down she gazes at the Weaving Maid and Herdboy stars

known for his concern with social injustice, feels bereft of access to the
royal presence and the means to effect change. The silver lantern (*chu,*
"candle," is a euphemism here for the celestial lanterns) is the moon, and
the chill is that of loneliness, not the weather—which is still hot this time
of year.

154

中秋月　蘇軾

暮雲收盡溢清寒　銀漢無聲轉玉盤
此生此夜不長好　明月明年何處看

Su Shih (1037–1101) wrote this poem in 1078 while serving as prefect of Hsuchou on the Grand Canal. He was joined on this occasion by his younger brother, Su Ch'e (1039–1112), with whom he had an unusually close relationship. Both brothers held numerous posts during their careers, and they spent much of their lives out of favor and far from the capital and their families. Still, as the last line suggests, both brothers made every effort to be together on this night, which was the eighth full moon and second in importance only to the lunar New Year as a time of family celebration. The wheel of jade that moves through the sky is the moon, and the Silver River, also known as the Long River or River of Heaven, is the Milky Way. Su composed this poem to be sung to the tune of "Yang Pass."

Mid-Autumn Moon

SU SHIH

As evening clouds withdraw a clear cool air floods in
the jade wheel passes silently across the Silver River
this life this night has rarely been kind
where will we see this moon next year

155

江樓有感　趙嘏

獨上江樓思悄然　月光如水水如天
同來玩月人何在　風景依稀似去年

Chao Ku (815–856) was born in Huai-an in Kiangsu province. After passing the civil service exam in 842, he served in a number of posts and finally as commandant of Weinan, to which he eventually retired. Weinan is located on the south shore of the Wei River just east of Ch'ang-an and served as the capital's entrepôt for goods coming up the Yellow River. Towers were built along rivers in China to monitor boat traffic. But they were also used for enjoying the view, especially on moonlit nights. Tu Mu (803–852) was so taken with the line in another Chao Ku poem ("I lean from a tower listening to a flute"), he gave Chao the nickname "Tower Leaning Chao."

Reflections at a River Tower

CHAO KU

Alone on a river tower my thoughts full of sorrow
the moonlight like the water the water like the sky
where is the person with whom I shared the moon
the view isn't quite the same as last year

156

題臨安邸　林升

山外青山樓外樓　西湖歌舞幾時休
煖風薰得遊人醉　直把杭州作汴州

Lin Sheng (fl. 1180) was a native of Putien in Fukien province. Lin witnessed the transfer of the Sung capital from Pienchou (Kaifeng) in North China to Linan (Hangchou) south of the Yangtze, and here he describes the carefree decadence of the new Sung capital and laments the lack of concern among the émigré officials and nobles for the loss of the old capital to the Khitan Tartars. The Khitans destroyed Pienchou in 1127 and the Sung court fled south, first to Nanching and then, when Nanching proved too difficult to defend, to Hangchou, which was renamed Linan and made the new capital in 1129. It is now more than fifty years later, and who thinks of returning to Kaifeng? But the last line is not only a lamentation; it is also a warning. Hangchou's West Lake was surrounded on three sides by hills, and its shores were lined with one pavilion after another. Its most famous lakeshore restaurant is still called Lou-Wai-Lou (Pavilion Beyond Pavilions).

Written at an Inn in Linan

LIN SHENG

Hills upon hills pavilions beyond pavilions
the singing and dancing never stop at West Lake
revelers are so drunk on the warmth
they mistake Hangchou for Pienchou

157

曉出淨慈寺送林子方　楊萬里

畢竟西湖六月中　風光不與四時同
接天蓮葉無窮碧　映日荷花別樣紅

Yang Wan-li (1124–1206) was from Kiangsi province and served in a number of minor posts in the provinces and in the capital of Hangchou. While serving as prefect of the Grand Canal town of Changchou, he came to a new understanding of poetic technique that he equated with the enlightenment of Zen. He threw away his earlier work and began writing a dozen or more new poems every day. When he died he left behind over 20,000 poems, of which some 4,000 are still extant. Chingtzu Temple was one of the largest Buddhist monasteries in Hangchou and was located on the south shore of West Lake. Yang's friend Lin Tzu-fang had been serving in the capital's Palace Library but is leaving on some unspecified journey. Lotus leaves rise four or five feet above the water on long stems, and their flowers, which are various shades of pink, rise to about the same height before opening.

At Chingtzu Temple Seeing Off Lin Tzu-fang at Dawn

YANG WAN-LI

Finally West Lake in the month of July
the scene isn't like any other time of year
sky-high lotus leaves are an endless blue-green
and their sunlit flowers are a different kind of red

158

飲湖上初晴後雨　蘇軾

水光瀲灩晴方好　山色空濛雨亦奇
欲把西湖比西子　淡粧濃抹總相宜

Su Shih (1037–1101) wrote this poem in 1073 when he was serving as controller-general of Hangchou, which would not become the capital of the Southern Sung for another fifty years. Hsi-tzu (Western Beauty) was another name for Hsi Shih, a famous beauty of the state of Yueh. Following a disastrous defeat by the state of Wu in 494 B.C., the King of Yueh (r. 496–465 B.C.) gave Hsi Shih to the King of Wu in hopes that she would distract him from state affairs, an assignment in which she succeeded famously. As a result of this poem, some people started calling West Lake "Western Beauty Lake." According to an account in *Lengchi yehhua*, "When Tung-p'o [Su Shih's pen name] was serving in Hangchou, there was not a day he did not visit West Lake."

Drinking on the Lake As It Clears Then Rains

SU SHIH

The shimmering waves are translucent when it clears
the mist-veiled hills are transcendent when it rains
I think of West Lake as the Beauty of the West
equally lovely in powder or paint

159

入直召對選德殿賜茶而退　周必大

綠槐夾道集昏鴉　敕使傳宣坐賜茶

歸到玉堂清不寐　月鈎初上紫薇花

Chou Pi-ta (1126–1204) was from Chi-an in Kiangsi province. As an offi-
cial, he was known for his unflinching honesty and willingness to criticize
policies he thought harmful. On this occasion, which would have been
one of the great events in any official's life, he was summoned to a private
audience with Emperor Hsiao-tsung (r. 1163–1189). At the time, Chou was
serving in the Hanlin Academy, which was in charge of preparing official
documents. It was also called Jade Hall, and during the T'ang, when it was
in Ch'ang-an, it acquired the appellation Purple Myrtle Court, after the
flowers planted around its courtyard and along the walkways outside. Af-
ter returning from his audience Chou sees in the crescent moon his own
prospects waxing as well. In 1189 he was appointed deputy prime minister;
hence, this poem would have been written sometime earlier. Pagoda trees
(*Sophora japonica*) were known for their shade and also for their pagoda-
like panicles of fragrant yellow blossoms that bloomed during summer.

Retiring After Attending a Tea at Hsuante Palace

CHOU PI-TA

Pagoda trees crowd the path crows flock at dusk
a messenger brings a summons to a tea
returning to Jade Hall how can I sleep
with a new crescent moon above the myrtle

Thus, they were often planted in front of temples and palaces whenever a
deciduous tree was favored over an evergreen. The crows also refer to
black-robed officials returning from the palace.

160

夏日登車蓋亭　蔡確

紙屏石枕竹方床　手倦拋書午夢長

睡起莞然成獨笑　數聲漁笛在滄浪

Ts'ai Ch'ueh (1037–1093) was from Chuanchou in Fukien province. He rose to the rank of minister during the reign of Emperor Shen-tsung (r. 1068–1085) and at first supported Wang An-shih's financial reforms. But when the emperor changed sides, so did Ts'ai. In addition to his opportunism, he was also known for his arrogance, and he delighted in harassing others. He was later appointed prefect of Anlu in Hupei province and wrote a series of ten poems while visiting this pavilion outside Anlu that overlooked a tributary of the Han River. When the military governor of Hanyang heard these poems, he took advantage of a few double entendres to balance accounts and accused Ts'ai of disrespect to the throne. Ts'ai was arrested and died in detention. Until modern times, Chinese preferred porcelain or stone pillows during summer, as they "cool the brain." Mats of woven bamboo or rattan are also used in the summer to reduce the body's heat. And a square bed is meant to be shared. The fisherman here recalls the figure

Climbing to Canopy Pavilion on a Summer Day

TS'AI CH'UEH

A paper screen a stone pillow a square bamboo bed
a book falls from my hand during a midday dream
I wake up pleased and smile to myself
at the sound of a fisherman's flute on the waves

in the poem titled "The Fisherman" in the *Chutzu*, in which a fisherman
criticizes Ch'u Yuan (340–278 B.C.) for his rigid adherence to principle and
rows away singing: "When the waves are clear I wash my hat [serve in
office] / when the waves are muddy I wash my feet [retire]."

161

直玉堂作　洪咨夔

禁門深鎖寂無譁　濃墨淋漓兩相麻
唱徹五更天未曉　一墀月浸紫薇花

Hung Tzu-k'uei (1176–1235) was a native of the Hangchou area. In addition to serving as vice-minister of justice, he also served as a scholar in the Hanlin Academy, which was also known as Jade Hall. The Academy was in charge of drafting edicts for the emperor's approval, in this case, the edict appointing the chief ministers empowered to oversee government affairs. On such an occasion, members of the Hanlin Academy would have stayed up all night in order to have the appointments ready for the emperor's vermilion seal at the predawn audience. The poet pauses to savor the hour before the sun rises, as the moon sets on the purple myrtle lining the steps and courtyard outside the Academy.

Written While Serving at Jade Hall

HUNG TZU-K'UEI

The forbidden gates are locked and silent
thick ink soaks ministerial appointments
the crier announces the last watch before dawn
moonlight floods the myrtle-lined steps

162

南風不用蒲葵扇　紗帽閒眠對水鷗
傲吏身閒笑五侯　西江取竹起高樓

竹樓　李嘉祐

Li Chia-yu (719–781) was a native of Chaohsien in Hopei province and the uncle of Li Tuan, who was one of the Ten Talents of the Tali Period. He served as a proofreader in the Palace Library, but due to some unspecified offense he was banished to the South. Although he was called back to the capital, he didn't stay long and was sent back to the provinces, where he served as magistrate of a series of prefectures south of the Yangtze. The phrase "upright official" (*ao-li*) comes from the story about Chuang-tzu in Ssu-ma Ch'ien's biography of him, in which the Taoist sage refuses the post of prime minister in favor of a minor post near his hometown north of Minchuan on the Honan–Shantung border. Here, the phrase refers to Secretary Wang, whose job would have been to draft documents in some government office. The tower Wang built was intended as a sleeping platform during the hot and humid Yangtze summer. The South Wind is the wind of compassionate government, but it also represents the less severe

Written at Secretary Wang's Bamboo Tower

LI CHIA-YU

An idle upright official laughs at the high and mighty
west of the river he built a tower of bamboo
who needs a palm leaf when the South Wind blows
wearing his silk hat he naps beside gulls

cultural milieu south of the Yangtze. An ancient poem goes: "The touch of
the South Wind can relieve my people's pains." Li also recalls a story in
Liehtzu (2.11) in which gulls are said to perceive the thoughts of those
who might want to harm or catch them. Clearly, this official has no such
thoughts. Also, although he is "idle" and thus not currently employed, he
still wears his hat, the emblem of office, suggesting his readiness to serve
should the occasion arise.

163

直中書省　白居易

絲綸閣下文章靜　鐘鼓樓中刻漏長
獨坐黃昏誰是伴　紫薇花對紫薇郎

Pai Chu-yi (772–846), aka Pai Le-t'ien, was born across the Yellow River from Loyang but grew up east of Ch'ang-an near Weinan. A man of high principle, he fell out of favor early in his career and was banished to Kiangsi, where he served as that province's military commissioner. When he was called back to Ch'ang-an he refused to take sides in court politics and asked instead to be sent back to the provinces to serve as prefect of Hangchou and then Suchou. This poem was written in 821 after he returned to Ch'ang-an. Gossamer Hall (Ssulunko) was another name for the building where imperial decrees were drafted and where Pai was serving as Minister of Justice. However, at this time the real power at court was in the hands of the eunuchs—hence, the lack of decrees to draft. Pai identified with the sufferings of the common people. But having failed to achieve any reforms that might have helped their lot, he is simply waiting for another day at the ministry to end. He eventually retired from government

Serving in the Secretariat

PAI CHU-YI

At Gossamer Hall the writing has stopped
the hours drip slowly in the bell and drum towers
sitting here at dusk who are my companions
purple myrtle flowers face a purple myrtle man

service and spent his remaining years in the company of the monks at
Hsiangshan Temple, across from the Lungmen Caves south of Loyang. His
grave is still there, facing the big stone buddha carved to resemble Empress
Wu Tse-t'ien. Periods of time at court were calculated using a water clock
and were announced by a huge bell and an even bigger drum in the twin
towers just inside the main gate of the imperial courtyard. As noted pre-
viously, purple myrtle was planted extensively around the courtyard of the
Secretariat and bloomed from mid-June until the end of September.

164

觀書有感（一）　朱熹

半畝方塘一鑑開　天光雲影共徘徊
問渠那得清如許　為有源頭活水來

Chu Hsi (1130–1200) was born in Fukien province, but he spent most of his life elsewhere. After a precocious childhood he served in a series of provincial posts and academic positions in the central government in Hangchou. But he was better known as one of the great neo-Confucian writers and philosophers of the Sung dynasty. On this occasion he incorporates his philosophy of the mind in a poem about a pond. The Chinese called the mind the "square-inch" (*fang-ts'un*). Here, like a Chinese bronze mirror kept covered until needed, the mind opens to reflect the world of light and dark, sunshine and clouds. And like a pond, it is constantly refreshed by the inexhaustible water of the Tao.

Reflections While Reading—1

CHU HSI

A small square pond an uncovered mirror
where sunlight and clouds linger and leave
I asked how it stays so clear
it said spring water keeps flowing in

165

觀書有感（二）　朱熹

昨夜江邊春水生　艨艟巨艦一毛輕
向來枉費推移力　此日中流自在行

In writing this poem, Chu Hsi probably had the first chapter of *Chuang-tzu* in mind, in which the Taoist sage says, "Pouring a cupful of water into a depression, a mustard seed can serve as a boat. But if you place the cup in the water, it gets stuck. The water is too shallow, and the boat too large." Like Chuang-tzu, Chu Hsi preferred to express his philosophy through metaphor rather than abstraction. Here, his point is that an understanding of the Tao does not depend so much on an expenditure of effort as it does on an awareness of the nature of change. These particular warships were covered in leather in order to withstand projectiles and were used during battles to ram other ships. Thus, they were quite heavy.

Reflections While Reading—II

CHU HSI

Last night spring waters rose along the river
even great warships seemed light as a feather
trying to row earlier would have been useless
today in midstream they travel with ease

166

冷泉亭　林禛

一泓清可沁詩脾　冷煖年來只自知
流出西湖載歌舞　回頭不似在山時

Lin Chen (fl. 1180) was from Suchou in Kiangsu province but has left
us no other information about himself than what can be gathered from
this poem. Some commentators attribute this poem to another Lin Chen
(fl. 1050) from Fukien province. The last couplet, however, suggests it was
written after the Sung court moved to Hangchou, which would support
the attribution to the later man. Still others assign the poem to a man
named Lin Hung, about whom nothing else is known. In any case, Cold
Spring Pavilion was at the foot of a rock formation in Hangchou known
as Feilai Peak, opposite the front gate of Lingyen Temple. From here, the
spring flows along a rocky bed for several kilometers and then empties
into the northwest corner of West Lake. Following the relocation of the
court to Hangchou in 1129, West Lake became the scene of constant parties
by an expatriate government that lacked the will or the power to retake
North China from the Khitans. Lin, like most Chinese, accepted Mencius's

Cold Spring Pavilion

LIN CHEN

A stream of pure water can soothe a poet's soul
it alone knows how warm or cold the years have been
flowing into West Lake it carries entertainers
looking back it's changed since the mountains

view (*Mencius*: 6b.8) that our nature is originally pure but becomes im-
pure as the result of improper involvement in our social and cultural
environment, and also because of poor nourishment. When Zen masters
try to explain enlightenment to their disciples, they often compare it to
drinking water: "Whether it's warm or cold is something you have taste
for yourself."

167

贈劉景文　蘇軾

荷盡已無擎雨蓋　菊殘猶有傲霜枝
一年好景君須記　最是橙黃橘綠時

Su Shih (1037–1101) wrote this poem in 1090 when he was out of favor and had been sent to Hangchou as the city's prefect. Earlier, Su had become close friends with Liu (1033–1092) when Su was rusticated to the same area in 1080. Liu was from Kaifeng and was serving as commander-in-chief of military forces in the province of which Hangchou was the capital. The two men became such close friends that Su compared Liu to K'ung Jung (153–208), a Han-dynasty Confucian noted for his erudition and courage. Among the many poems the two men exchanged in later years was this one, in which Su reminds his friend of their time together in Hangchou and of the region's citrus trees, which produced their fruit long after the flowers of summer and fall had faded and after all other fruits had been harvested. Such fruit is also a metaphor for the pleasures of old age.

For Liu Ching-wen

SU SHIH

Lotuses are gone and their rainproof umbrellas
chrysanthemums have faded but not their hardy leaves
the year's best scene though surely you'll recall
is when oranges are yellow and tangerines are green

168

楓橋夜泊　張繼

月落烏啼霜滿天　江楓漁火對愁眠
姑蘇城外寒山寺　夜半鐘聲到客船

Chang Chi (fl. 760) was born in Hsiangfanyang in Hupei province. During the Tali Period (766–779), he served in Ch'ang-an as vice-director of the Bureau of Sacrifices and later in Nanchang as assistant commissioner of the Salt and Iron Monopoly Bureau, where he is said to have died. Here, he is traveling along the Grand Canal and has moored for the night in the western suburbs of Suchou. The bridge where he dropped anchor was named Feng Ch'iao (Enfeoffment Bridge), but Chang chose the more auspicious homophone *feng* (maple). As a result of the popularity of this poem — and it is perhaps the most famous poem in the Chinese language — the name of the bridge was changed. It's still there, a few hundred meters north of Hanshan Temple. Although most accounts claim the temple was named for the reclusive poet Han-shan (Cold Mountain), Han-shan was Chang's contemporary and his poetry did not become well known until the end of the next century. The temple was actually named for a nearby hill. Temple

Anchored Overnight at Maple Bridge

CHANG CHI

Crows caw the moon sets frost fills the sky
river maples fishing fires care-plagued sleep
coming from Cold Mountain Temple outside the Suchou wall
the sound of the midnight bell reaches a traveler's boat

bells were seldom rung so late, but it was customary in Suchou and else-
where during the T'ang to ring the "Bell of Impermanence" at midnight.
The river maples recall the final lines of Ch'u Yuan's (340–278 B.C.) "Call-
ing Back the Soul": "On and on the river flows / maple trees line the shore
/ I wish I could see for a thousand miles / but my spring heart breaks in
sorrow / O soul come back / I grieve for the lands of the South." Fisher-
men used lanterns and torches at night to attract fish, and cormorants to
catch them.

169

寒夜　杜耒

寒夜客來茶當酒
竹爐湯沸火初紅
尋常一樣窗前月
纔有梅花便不同

Tu Lei (d. 1240) was from Linchuan in Kiangsi province. Toward the end of his life he served as private secretary to Hsu Kuo, the minister of the imperial treasury. However, on a mission to Shantung he was killed along with his superior by General Li Ch'uan. When the Chinese first began drinking tea in the fifth and sixth centuries, they boiled it along with ingredients as diverse as cloves and scallions and drank it mostly as a medicinal broth. It wasn't until the ninth and tenth centuries that they began drinking tea by itself—though as a powder they whisked into boiling water rather than in the form of leaves. This small, portable tea stove was made of clay and included a woven bamboo exterior that allowed it to be moved about while the coals inside it were still hot. Only a close friend would appreciate such simple pleasures. And only such a friend, who no doubt also came to appreciate a friend's plum blossoms, would visit on such a night.

Winter Night

TU LEI

> For a winter-night guest tea serves as wine
> boiling on a wicker stove as the coals turn red
> outside the window is the same old moon
> but with plum blossoms now it's different

170

霜月　李商隱

初聞征雁已無蟬　百尺樓高水接天

青女素娥俱耐冷　月中霜裏鬥嬋娟

Li Shang-yin (813–858) was born in Chinyang in Honan province and grew up in Chengchou and Loyang. He was considered one of the best poets of his day, and he is still ranked among the great poets of the T'ang. He was related through marriage and friendship to the two competing factions at court led by Li Te-yu and Niu Seng-ju; unable to resolve the contradictions in his relationships, he eventually incurred the enmity of his friend Ling-hu T'ao (802–879), who held the position of prime minister and who made it impossible for Li to serve in anything but minor posts. Li died without office in Chengchou. Here, he cloaks these factions in the guise of two celestial maidens. After ingesting a magic elixir, Ch'ang O floated up to the moon and has been its resident goddess ever since. Ch'ing Nu, whose name means "Girl from the Blue," is the Goddess of Frost. According to the *Lichi* (*Book of Rites*), "In the first month of fall, the cold cicadas sing. In the second month of fall, the geese fly past. In the

The Frost and the Moon

LI SHANG-YIN

By the time I hear geese the cicadas are gone
from a hundred-foot tower the water is like the sky
Ch'ang O and Ch'ing Nu don't mind the cold
in the frost and moonlight they contest each other's charms

third month of fall, the frost begins to fall" (6). Viewed from afar, the
moonlit water of Ch'ang O and the frost-filled sky of Ch'ing Nu don't ap-
pear different, their claims notwithstanding. So, too, are the two factions
at court equally deserving of praise but also of criticism for their narrow-
minded views of one another.

171

梅　王淇

不受塵埃半點侵
竹籬茅舍自甘心
只因誤識林和靖
惹得詩人說到今

Wang Ch'i (c. 1150) has left no information about himself other than what can be gathered from a few surviving poems. Ever since Lin Pu (967–1028), aka Lin Ho-ching, began singing the praises of the plum blossom, the flower came to represent a life of simplicity and beauty in the face of adversity. Especially famous were his lines: "Its scattered shadows fall lightly on clear water / its subtle scent pervades the moonlit dusk." But Wang is concerned that as a result of Lin's infatuation with the plum, others now exhaust themselves trying to excel him, and that more often than not they fail to understand or to cultivate the plum's true spirit of purity and simplicity. Lin lived as a recluse on a small island at the edge of Hang-chou's West Lake when the city was still a provincial backwater, long before it became the capital of the Southern Sung dynasty. He never sought public office, never married, and amused himself by teaching cranes to dance. People say the plum was his wife, and the cranes were his children.

The Plum

WANG CH'I

Immune from the slightest contaminating dust
content beside a thatched hut or bamboo fence
then you met Lin Pu by mistake
poets ever since haven't stopped talking

172

早春　白玉蟾

南枝纔放兩三花　雪裏吟香弄粉些
淡淡著煙濃著月　深深籠水淺籠沙

Pai Yu-ch'an (fl. 1195–1230), aka Ko Ch'ang-keng, was born on Hainan Island in South China and became a Taoist priest at an early age. After studying with various masters, he finally settled in the Wuyi Mountains of Fukien province. He is ranked as the Fifth Patriarch of the Southern School of Taoism and composed a number of well-known works on inner alchemy. He was also known for his calligraphy and painting. In this poem he uses the southernmost tip of a plum branch to pinpoint the end of winter and the first sign of spring. In the second line he likens the plum blossom to a woman wearing perfume and makeup. And in the last two lines he views the blossoms under different conditions and with different backdrops. The wording of these last two lines is indebted to Tu Mu's "Anchored Overnight on the Chinhuai" (verse 176). In the second line, the word *fen* can mean "powder" as well as "pollen," and most commentators interpret it as referring to the blossom's powdery appearance. But as the

Early Spring

PAI YU-CH'AN

As soon as a southern branch unveils its first buds
I savor the perfume and pollen in the snow
paler in the mist whiter in the moonlight
darker on the water lighter on the sand

great plum connoisseur Sung Po-jen notes in the introduction to his *Guide to Capturing a Plum Blossom*, "I breathe on their petals, inhale their fragrance, and taste their pollen."

173

雪梅（一）　盧梅坡

梅雪爭春未肯降　騷人閣筆費評章
梅須遜雪三分白　雪卻輸梅一段香

Lu Mei-p'o (Sung dynasty) has left nothing behind but these two poems. The name by which he was known means Plum Tree Slope and, no doubt, was a pen name. Some editions attribute these poems to Fang Yueh (1198–1262), who was a native of Chihsien in Anhui province. Either way, they are good examples of the Chinese poet's view of his art. In this first poem the poet demonstrates that there are no absolutes. Everything has its own incomparable quality. But this leaves us with a conundrum: in a world where everything is unique, what can we use as a standard, and how can we speak of beauty?

The Snow and the Plum—1

LU MEI-P'O

The plum and the snow both claim the spring
a poet gives up trying to decide
the plum must admit the snow is three times whiter
but the snow can't match a wisp of plum perfume

174

雪梅（二）　盧梅坡

有梅無雪不精神　有雪無詩俗了人
日暮詩成天又雪　與梅並作十分春

In this second verse the poet resolves his conundrum by introducing the poem—and thus the poet—as the catalyst that transforms the separate worlds of the plum and the snow into one world of beauty. Thus, the poet justifies his existence as well as his passion by his ability to perceive the spirit and the appearance of things without dividing one from the other, which is what a poem aims to do.

The Snow and the Plum—II

LU MEI-P'O

The plum without the snow isn't very special
and snow without a poem is simply commonplace
at sunset when the poem is done then it snows again
together with the plum they complete the spring

175

牧童　呂洞賓

草鋪橫野六七里
笛弄晚風三四聲
歸來飽飯黃昏後
不脫蓑衣臥月明

Lu Tung-pin (fl. 870) was from Yunglo in Shansi province. After failing to pass the civil service exam, he met Chung-li Ch'uan (aka Han Chung-li) at a wineshop in Ch'ang-an, got drunk, realized the impermanence of human existence, and joined Chung-li in leading a group of Taoists who became known as the Eight Immortals. In some texts, such as Hu Tzu's *Tiaohsi yuyin tsunghua* (pub. 1148), this poem is entitled "In Reply to Chung Juo-weng," and the author is listed as "a herdboy." Chung (fl. 1105) was an otherwise unremarkable scholar from Kiangsi province who received an appointment to the Palace Library in Kaifeng as the result of a recommendation and was subsequently dismissed for issuing false reports of military successes. Although Chung was clearly in need of the advice offered by this poem, I have, instead, gone along with the *Chuantangshih*, which attributes the poem to Lu Tung-pin and entitles it "Herdboy." In either case, it presents the Taoist vision of the well-lived life of a person at

Herdboy

LU TUNG-PIN

Across the countryside grass spreads for miles
I blow a few notes on the evening wind
back home I eat after the sun sets
and lie in the moonlight still wearing my raincoat

peace with the world and in harmony with its changes. In South China, farmers wove their raincoats from the bark of the coir palm (*Trachycarpus excelsa*). In North China, where Lu lived, they used a coat of woven reeds in summer and one of animal skins in winter.

176

秦淮夜泊　杜牧

煙籠寒水月籠沙
夜泊秦淮近酒家
商女不知亡國恨
隔江猶唱後庭花

Tu Mu (803–852) grew up in Ch'ang-an in a prestigious family that had fallen on hard times, and his only posts of significance were those he held during his rustications. Here, he drops anchor on the Chinhuai River outside Nanching's South Gate. The river also acted as the city's moat before it joined the Yangtze a dozen kilometers to the west, and this was where many of those visiting the city disembarked. Along the moat's south shore were the "willow-lined lanes" of brothels and inns that catered to travelers and merchants. And behind the city wall on the north shore was the site of the Ch'en-dynasty (557–588) palace, which had since become a residential area for the rich and powerful. From one such home, Tu Mu hears the song "Rear Palace Flowers on a Tree of Jade" (*Yushu houtingkunghua*), which was composed by Ch'en Hou-chu (r. 583–588), who drank away his throne and brought the Ch'en dynasty to an end. Hearing it still sung, and, no doubt, the lines, "Rear palace flowers on a tree of jade / don't

Anchored Overnight on the Chinhuai

TU MU

Vapor shrouds the icy water moonlight shrouds the sand
I anchor near a brothel on the Chinhuai for the night
oblivious of the sorrow from a dynasty's demise
across the moat girls still sing "Rear Palace Flowers"

bloom again for a long long time," Tu Mu can only sigh that its lessons
have fallen on deaf ears. The eunuchs were now the real power behind the
throne, and most of Northern China had, in effect, become a number of
separate kingdoms.

177

歸雁　錢起

瀟湘何事等閒回　水碧沙明兩岸苔
二十五絃彈夜月　不勝清怨卻飛來

Ch'ien Ch'i (722–780) was from Huchou in Chekiang province but he spent most of his adult life in the Ch'ang-an area, where he served as a bureau director in the Ministry of Personnel and as an academician in the Hanlin Academy. Included among the Ten Talents of the Tali Period (766–779), he was considered a poetic successor to Wang Wei and Meng Hao-jan. Here, he asks wild geese why they turn around when they reach the Hsiao and Hsiang Rivers in southern Hunan province, where the environment seems so welcoming. The answer is the spiritual malaise of the region. When Emperor Fu Hsi (c. 2850 B.C.) heard the fifty-string zither, the sound so saddened him that he ordered the instrument limited to twenty-five strings, which are being played here by the two sisters both of whom married Emperor Shun (c. 2250 B.C.). When their husband died in battle south of Hunan, they drowned themselves where the Hsiang flows through Tungting Lake and became the river's and the lake's resident spirits. Two

On Geese Turning Back

CH'IEN CH'I

Why do they turn back when they reach the Hsiao and Hsiang
the water is green the sand is bright and both shores are mossy
twenty-five strings echo beneath the moon at night
unable to bear such melancholy they all fly away

thousand years later they were joined in the same river by Ch'u Yuan
(340–278 B.C.), whose suicide in the Milo River, which also empties into
Tungting Lake, is still commemorated by the Dragon Boat Festival on the
fifth day of the fifth month. The Hsiao flows into the Hsiang, and the
phrase *Hsiao-Hsiang* simply indicates their combined watershed. I've read
yeh-yueh (night moon) as descriptive. But it could also be taken as the
name of a song for the zither. Or it could even refer to the pavilion of that
name outside Yiyang, where the Hsiang joins Tungting Lake. In any case,
while such melancholy drives off the geese, exiled officials must wait to
be recalled.

題壁　無名氏

一團茅草亂蓬蓬　驀地燒天驀地空
爭似滿爐煨榾柮　漫騰騰地煖烘烘

In his *Kueierchi*, Chang Jui-yi quotes this poem and says it was written on the wall of a Buddhist temple on the sacred peak of Sungshan east of Loyang. According to Hsu Yen-chou's *Choushihhua*, when Ssu-ma Kuang (1019–1086) saw this poem there, he wrote "Don't erase this poem," then added: "When you're climbing a mountain, if you walk slowly, you won't become exhausted. And if you keep your feet on solid ground, you won't get hurt." Although this poem was ostensibly written to remind pilgrims and passersby of the true focus of spiritual practice, Ssu-ma Kuang saw in it a commentary on the complex, radical economic reforms of Wang Anshih, and many commentators have agreed with him. Like many similar poems in this collection, it probably would not have been included if it had not been open to such double entendre.

Written on a Wall

AUTHOR UNKNOWN

A pile of dry rushes in total disarray
suddenly lights the sky and suddenly is gone
no match for a stove full of old stump wood
slowly steadily giving off heat

PART FOUR

179

早朝大明宮　賈至

銀燭朝天紫陌長　禁城春色曉蒼蒼
千條弱柳垂青瑣　百囀流鶯繞建章
劍佩聲隨玉墀步　衣冠身惹御爐香
共沐恩波鳳池上　朝朝染翰侍君王

Chia Chih (718–772) was born in Loyang and enjoyed a distinguished career under several emperors, all of whom admired his skill in polishing their edicts, a skill he inherited from his father, who served in the same capacity. The son wrote this in late spring of 758 while serving in the Secretariat under Emperor Su-tsung. Although written as a court poem, it was such a good example of the genre that several colleagues responded in the same vein (three such poems follow). Taming Palace housed the royal family and highest offices of the central government in Ch'ang-an. Built on the site of the Han dynasty's Chienchang Court, it also retained the earlier name. In the first line, courtiers light the sky with their lanterns as they proceed by carriage to the palace. Phoenix Pond was just outside the Secretariat.

Morning Court at Taming Palace

CHIA CHIH

Silver lanterns light the sky along imperial streets
in spring forbidden walls turn bright green at dawn
countless hanging catkins veil the painted gates
a hundred twittering orioles encircle Chienchang Court
the sounds of swords and pendants echo up jade steps
every robe and hat is lined with incense soot
and bathed in waves of grace at Phoenix Pond
and daily stained with ink in the service of our lord

180

和賈舍人早朝大明宮　杜甫

五夜漏聲催曉箭　九重春色醉仙桃
旌旗日煖龍蛇動　宮殿風微燕雀高
朝罷香煙攜滿袖　詩成珠玉任揮毫
欲知世掌絲綸美　池上於今有鳳毛

Not long after Emperor Su-tsung's return to Ch'ang-an in 757, Tu Fu (712–770) was reappointed censor but was demoted the next year. The water clock's arrow indicated when it was time for court, and the sleeves of Chinese robes were like wings. "Gossamer" refers to the emperor's silken and never-ending edicts. Tu Fu likens Chia Chih to Hsieh Chao-tsung (whose name meant "phoenix"), who also followed his father in composing imperial edicts, and of whom Emperor Wu (r. 502–549) of the Liang dynasty said, "You are so capable, you must have phoenix feathers." The feather here is Chia Chih's poem.

Responding to Secretary Chia Chih's "Morning Court at Taming Palace"

TU FU

The sound of nightlong dripping speeds the shaft of dawn
spring within the inner gates intoxicates the peach trees
dragons writhe on tapestries in the warming sun
tiny birds soar above on the faintest breeze
incense spills from our sleeves after court
pearls pour from your brush into a poem
how do generations learn such gossamer art
by the pond today I found a phoenix feather

181

和賈舍人早朝大明宮　王維

絳幘雞人報曉籌　尚衣方進翠雲裘
九天閶闔開宮殿　萬國衣冠拜冕旒
日色纔臨仙掌動　香煙欲傍袞龍浮
朝罷須裁五色詔　佩聲歸到鳳池頭

Wang Wei (701–761) was reappointed to the Secretariat in 758 and became its deputy director the following year. The dawn crier wore a red cap to mimic a rooster and announced dawn by beating bamboo on a wooden board. The steward was in charge of dressing the emperor, and nine is the number of levels of Heaven. At morning court, two huge fans were held behind the emperor to block the rising sun. Also, the bottom of his robe was decorated with nine dragons playing with the sun and moon. After court, Chia Chih and the other members of the Secretariat returned to their offices to prepare documents generated by the morning audience, which they wrote on multicolored paper. As they went about their duties, the pendants attached to their sashes chimed.

Responding to Secretary Chia Chih's "Morning Court at Taming Palace"

WANG WEI

When the crimson-capped crier strikes the dawn clapper
the royal steward enters with azure cloud robes
the ninefold gates of the palace swing open
courtiers from every land bow before the throne
then the sun rises and celestial fans wave
incense smoke swirls beside dragon brocade
after court flowery decrees must be drafted
the sound of jade pendants returns to Phoenix Pond

182

和賈舍人早朝大明宮　岑參

雞鳴紫陌曙光寒　鶯囀皇州春色闌
金闕曉鐘開萬戶　玉階仙仗擁千官
花迎劍佩星初落　柳拂旌旗露未乾
獨有鳳凰池上客　陽春一曲和更難

Ts'en Shen (715–770) was from Chiangling in the middle reaches of the Yangtze. After beginning his career as a military aide on the Silk Road, he returned to Ch'ang-an as part of Emperor Su-tsung's entourage in 757 and was serving as rectifier of omissions when he wrote this response. Swords and pendants were worn at the waist, and the banners accompanied different administrative units. The scene in the second half of the poem is that of officials returning to their offices after morning court. Phoenix Pond was just outside the Secretariat where Chia Chih and those who responded to his poem worked. "Yangchun" ("Sunny Spring") was the name of a tune that was too difficult for most people to sing.

Responding to Secretary Chia Chih's "Morning Court at Taming Palace"

TS'EN SHEN

Roosters announce dawn in the capital is cold
orioles proclaim spring in the royal realm is over
the golden gate's morning bell wakes ten thousand households
attendants line jade steps and crowd a thousand officials
pendants and swords reflect the fading stars
banners brush dew from the willows
how rare is the man at Phoenix Pond
and how hard to match his "Sunny Spring"

183

上元應制　蔡襄

高列千峰寶炬森　端門方喜翠華臨
列遊不為三元夜　樂事還同萬眾心
天上清光留此夕　人間和氣閣春陰
要知盡慶華封祝　四十餘年惠愛深

Ts'ai Hsiang (1012–1067) was from Hsienyu in Fukien province and rose to the rank of minister in the Ministry of Rites and the Department of State Affairs. He was also one of the greatest calligraphers of the Sung dynasty. This poem describes the first night of the first full moon of the year's first season, when Sung emperors traveled in a great procession down the main street of Kaifeng. Huafeng, east of Ch'ang-an, was where emperors performed sacrifices to the sacred mountain of Huashan to ensure the birth of sons, their own longevity, and the prosperity of their reign. Emperor Jen-tsung (r. 1023–1063) reigned for forty-one years, and this turned out to be his last lantern festival.

On Lantern Festival at Imperial Request

TS'AI HSIANG

A forest of jeweled candles forms a thousand peaks
the royal gate is graced by his iridescent presence
the procession isn't for the year's first moon
but for sharing the joy of the people
the sky's clear light lasts all night
the world's mild air foreshadows the spring
the reason all wish him the blessings of Huafeng
for more than forty years his benevolence has grown

184

上元應制　王珪

雪消華月滿仙臺　萬燭當樓寶扇開
雙鳳雲中扶輦下　六鰲海上駕山來
鎬京春酒霑周宴　汾水秋風陋漢才
一曲昇平人盡樂　君王又進紫霞杯

Wang Kuei (1019–1085) was from the Chengtu area of Szechuan. During the reigns of Jen-tsung (1023–1063) and Shen-tsung (1068–1085), he directed the Hall of Scholarly Worthies and also served as prime minister. Here, he describes a royal banquet celebrating the first full moon and the images meant to remind the audience of their host's immortal heritage. The two phoenixes are yoked to the celestial carriage of Hsi-wang-mu, Queen Mother of the West, dispenser of the elixir of immortality. And the three pairs of tortoises support three islands in the East Sea where immortals live. Wang also recalls similar feasts held during the Chou dynasty (1122–255 B.C.) at its capital of Hao and during the Han dynasty (206 B.C.–A.D. 220), when Emperor Wu (r. 140–87 B.C.) banqueted on the Fen River and wrote poems about the autumn wind. It was the royal custom to eat and drink more in good times and less in bad times. Hence, Wang hopes for another cup of wine.

On Lantern Festival at Imperial Request

WANG KUEI

It isn't snow but moonlight on the terrace of immortals
candles line the balconies and jeweled fans part
from the clouds two phoenixes lead a carriage down
from the sea six tortoises carry mountains in
spring wine in old Hao drenched the feasts of Chou
autumn wind on the Fen shamed the bards of Han
everyone rejoices in a song of lasting peace
may our lord lift up his rosy cup once more

185

侍宴安樂公主新宅應制　沈佺期

皇家貴主好神仙　別業初開雲漢邊
山出盡如鳴鳳嶺　池成不讓飲龍川
妝樓翠幌教春住　舞閣金鋪借日懸
侍從乘輿來此地　稱觴獻壽樂鈞天

Shen Ch'uan-ch'i (656–715) was from Neihuang in Honan province and served at the court of Empress Wu. Following her death in 705, he was accused of corruption and exiled to Vietnam but was soon recalled and served as a court poet under Chung-tsung (r. 705–710) and Jui-tsung (r. 710–712). Here, he records Chung-tsung's visit in 709 to the villa of his favorite daughter. The princess was as ambitious as Empress Wu and is said to have exceeded her in depravity and licentiousness. However, she was not as long-lived and was killed in 710 during a coup that led to the enthronement of Hsuan-tsung (r. 712–756). The River of Heaven was another name for the Milky Way. Singing Phoenix Ridge was in Shensi province, and Drinking Dragon Stream refers to a stretch of the Wei River just west of Ch'ang-an. But here both are meant to summon images of a Taoist paradise. "Chuntien Kuanglo" ("Joy Pervades Heaven") was an ancient court tune.

Attending a Banquet at the New Residence of Princess An-lo

SHEN CH'UAN-CH'I

Her Royal Highness loves immortals and gods
she built her estate near the River of Heaven
with hills like those of Singing Phoenix Ridge
and ponds that rival Drinking Dragon Stream
her green-curtained balconies invite the spring to stay
her gold-decked pavilions imitate the sun
as our imperial majesty's entourage arrives
she toasts his long life with "Joy Pervades Heaven"

186

答丁元珍　歐陽修

春風疑不到天涯　二月山城未見花
殘雪壓枝猶有橘　凍雷驚筍欲抽芽
夜聞啼雁生鄉思　病入新年感物華
曾是洛陽花下客　野芳雖晚不須嗟

Ou-yang Hsiu (1007–1072) was from Chi-an in Kiangsi province and was one of the great literary figures of his day as well as one of the leaders of government reform and, during his final years, opposition to the financial policies of Wang An-shih. Thus, he was banished on several occasions and wrote this poem in 1036 during his rustication as magistrate of Yichang at the mouth of the Yangtze Gorges. The man to whom this poem replies was serving in Yichang as district judge. Ou-yang Hsiu once served in Loyang, which was famous for its private gardens, and the "illness" to which he refers was probably the cause of his exile.

In Reply to Ting Yuan-chen

OU-YANG HSIU

Spring wind I guess doesn't reach this side of Heaven
this mountain town in March is still devoid of flowers
oranges still hang from snow-laden branches
dreaming bamboo shoots are startled by cold thunder
honking geese at night make me think of home
nursing last year's illness I feel the season's pulse
formerly a guest in the gardens of Loyang
why should I care if country plants bloom late

187

插花吟　邵雍

頭上花枝照酒卮　酒卮中有好花枝
身經兩世太平日　眼見四朝全盛時
況復筋骸粗康健　那堪時節正芳菲
酒涵花影紅光溜　爭忍花前不醉歸

Shao Yung (1011–1077) grew up in Yaohsien in Honan province. Instead of pursuing a career as an official, he devoted himself to neo-Confucian studies and lived as a farmer-recluse on Mount Sumen outside his hometown. He later moved to Loyang and was repeatedly offered positions at court in Kaifeng, all of which he refused, preferring to spend his time in the company of friends such as Ssu-ma Kuang. During the Sung, men wore their hair long and in a bun, and officials were required to wear hats. Hence, only those who were without a position or retired could afford to wear a few flowers for fun.

Flower Garland Song

SHAO YUNG

The flowers on my head shine in my cup
my cup contains beautiful flowers
I've seen two generations of peaceful days
and witnessed four reigns of prosperous times
then too my body is more or less sound
also the season is at the height of its bloom
my cup glows red with flower reflections
how can I face them and not go home drunk

188

寓意　晏殊

油壁香車不再逢　峽雲無跡任西東
梨花院落溶溶月　柳絮池塘淡淡風
幾日寂寥傷酒後　一番蕭索禁煙中
魚書欲寄何由達　水遠山長處處同

Yen Shu (991–1055) was from Fuchou in Kiangsi province. Despite growing up poor he managed to receive a good education, and his home in Kaifeng became a meeting place for the poets of his day. He eventually reached the post of prime minister. But only the ruthless hold power for long, and he spent his last decade in provincial posts. Here, he recalls an extramarital affair in late spring. The walls of a woman's carriage consisted of waterproof material, and the gorge clouds refer to the Sorceress of the Yangtze Gorges, whose name and cloud-wreathed image were associated with romantic liaisons, especially those that were impossible to maintain. Fires, even those for heating wine, were forbidden during the two days in April preceding Chingming, or Grave Sweeping Day.

Private Thoughts

YEN SHU

Her lacquered carriage no longer arrives
where do gorge clouds go when they vanish
a pear-blossom courtyard in waves of moonlight
a willow-lined pond in the lightest of winds
so many days of loneliness and drinking
and now desolation and no stove fire
I'd send a letter in a fish if I could
but everywhere rivers and mountains are endless

189

寒食　趙鼎

寂寂柴門村落裏　也教插柳紀年華
禁煙不到粵人國　上塚亦攜龐老家
漢寢唐陵無麥飯　山谿野徑有梨花
一樽竟藉青苔臥　莫管城頭奏暮笳

Chao Ting (1085–1147) was from Wenhsi in Shansi province and twice served as prime minister, but he incurred the wrath of the eunuch Ch'in Kuai and was banished to Chaochou on the southeast coast. Here, he notes the extent to which Chinese customs honoring ancestors were followed in this area where other ethnic groups such as the Yueh predominated. Willow wood was known for its regenerative power and was used to start the new fire after the two-day cooking ban. P'ang Te-kung (fl. 220) lived with his family on a mountain south of Hsiangyang, and his name was later linked with the custom of clearing weeds from one's ancestral grave. Chao, too, retreats to the countryside and tries to ignore the flute that reminds him of home. He died here soon afterwards as the result of a hunger strike.

Cold Food

CHAO TING

Over the most remote poorest village gate
people stick willow wood to mark the end of spring
in the Land of Yueh the fire ban's unknown
but like old P'ang they visit ancestral graves
here the royal tombs see no sign of grain
but mountain streams and paths are lined with fallen blossoms
after a jug of wine I lie down on the moss
and try to ignore the evening flute I hear on the city wall

190

清明　黃庭堅

佳節清明桃李笑　野田荒塚只生愁
雷驚天地龍蛇蟄　雨足郊原草木柔
人乞祭餘驕妾婦　士甘焚死不公侯
賢愚千載知誰是　滿眼蓬蒿共一坵

Huang T'ing-chien (1045–1105) was from Hsiushui in Kiangsi province. Despite the support of Su Shih, he did not enjoy a successful career and died in exile. Although he was considered Su's poetic heir, his style was unconventional and full of obscure allusions. Here, however, he recalls two well-known Chingming stories. The first is about a man who often came home drunk and told his wife he had been out with rich friends. His wife followed him the next day and watched him go from gravesite to gravesite begging for leftovers (*Mencius*: 4b/33.1). The second is about Chieh Chih-t'ui, who refused to serve Duke Wen (r. 635–628 B.C.). Even when the Duke set fire to the mountain he lived on, Chieh still refused and was burned to death. The Duke was so contrite, he began the practice of banning fire on the two days prior to Chingming.

Chingming

HUANG T'ING-CHIEN

Peach and plum trees smile on Chingming Day
weed-choked fields and graves can only sigh
thunder wakes the serpents in the earth and sky
rain fills the countryside with tender new plants
one begged for funeral scraps and tried to fool his wife
another died in flames rather than be enfeoffed
after a thousand years was the fool or wise man right
both share the same bramble-covered hills

191

清明日對酒　高翥

南北山頭多墓田　清門祭掃各紛然
紙灰飛作白蝴蝶　淚血染成紅杜鵑
日落狐狸眠塚上　夜歸兒女笑燈前
人生有酒須當醉　一滴何曾到九泉

Kao Chu (fl. 1200) was from Chekiang province and chose a life in the countryside outside his hometown of Yuyao over a career in Hangchou. A follower of the Rivers and Lakes school of poetry, he was called the Poetry King of Yuyao and his verses were often quoted in the capital. Here, he describes the scene when weeds are cleared from graves and paper money is burned to provide funds for departed spirits in the underworld. Because azaleas bloom during Chingming, they are planted around graves. Foxes often make their homes in coffins and are thought to be the transformed spirits of the dead. Just as the heavens were thought to have nine levels, the underworld inhabited by the dead also had nine levels, the first of which was marked by sulfur springs at the earth's surface.

Drinking Wine on Grave Sweeping Day

KAO CHU

Hillsides north and south are overrun with graves
sweeping rites on Chingming are nothing but a mess
paper ashes fly like snow-white butterflies
tears from broken hearts stain azaleas red
foxes sleep in tombs once the sun goes down
children play in lamplight on the way back home
who has wine this life should drink until they're drunk
no drop has ever reached the ninefold springs below

192

郊行即事　程顥

芳原綠野恣行時　春入遙山碧四圍
興逐亂紅穿柳巷　困臨流水坐苔磯
莫辭盞酒十分醉　祇恐風花一片飛
況是清明好天氣　不妨游衍莫忘歸

Ch'eng Hao (1032–1085) was from Loyang and served in Kaifeng as a companion to the crown prince and as an investigating censor. However, due to his opposition to the policies of Wang An-shih, he was demoted and sent to the southernmost part of the empire. He was later recalled but died on his way back. He and his younger brother, Ch'eng Yi, were major spokesmen for the neo-Confucian revival that dominated intellectual life in the Sung. Ch'eng Hao thought that separating the world into internal and external realities was the root of all ill, and that cultivating impartiality and spontaneity was the path all men should follow. In a letter to his fellow neo-Confucian Chang Tsai, he once wrote, "Why should a man think it wrong to follow things that are external, and right to seek what is internal?" He was a man for all seasons, not only spring.

Strolling outside Town

CH'ENG HAO

In the sweet green countryside I walk where I want
spring is in the distant hills jade on all four sides
inspired I chase every red down every willow lane
tired I sit on mossy rocks beside a rushing stream
don't refuse wine unless you're already drunk
fear only that flowers will leave with the wind
especially on Chingming when the weather is fine
why not go wandering just remember to return

193

畫架雙裁翠絡翻　佳人春戲小樓前
飄揚血色裙拖地　斷送玉容人上天
花板潤霑紅杏雨　綵繩斜挂綠楊煙
下來閑處從容立　疑是蟾宮謫降仙

鞦韆　僧惠洪

Hui-hung (1071–1128) was from Yifeng in Kiangsi province. Not much else is known about him other than that he was a Buddhist monk who lived at Chingliang Temple in Nanching. Clearly, he did not spend all his time in the meditation hall. The swing was introduced to the Chinese by northern nomads sometime during the first millennium B.C. For reasons I have yet to discover, it became part of the pastimes associated with Chingming, especially along the Yangtze in the land of Ch'u, where people usually stood rather than sat on the board. Toad Palace is another name for the moon, which is inhabited by a three-legged toad that is the transformation of Ch'ang O, Goddess of the Moon.

The Swing

HUI-HUNG

A pair of blue ropes swing from a painted frame
a beauty enjoys spring by a small pavilion
her crimson skirt flutters as it scrapes the ground
her beguiling jade face rises to the sky
the carved board glistens with apricot-blossom rain
colored ribbons trail in the green-willow haze
down she steps in silence and stands nonchalant
a banished immortal from Toad Palace it seems

194

曲江（一） 杜甫

一片花飛減卻春　風飄萬點正愁人
且看欲盡花經眼　莫厭傷多酒入唇
江上小堂巢翡翠　苑邊高塚臥麒麟
細推物理須行樂　何用浮名絆此身

Tu Fu (712–770) returned to Ch'ang-an at the end of 757 and was reappointed as a censor. But the post was merely a sinecure and he felt powerless to do anything to help the country recover from the An Lu-shan Rebellion. He wrote this and the next poem the following April while visiting the serpentine lake formed by an artificial canal that brought water from the Chungnan Mountains to the southeast corner of the capital. After passing the civil service exam in 752, Tu Fu and his fellow graduates were entertained by Emperor Hsuan-tsung at Purple Cloud Pavilion at the southwest corner of this waterway. But the pavilion and surrounding structures had since become home to kingfishers, which never nest near places frequented by humans, and the stone statues in front of the nearby grave mound of the Ch'in dynasty's Second Emperor had been knocked down.

While Drinking at the Chuchiang Waterway — 1

TU FU

Each flying petal diminishes the spring
ten thousand on the wind break a person's heart
watching the final flowers fall before my eyes
how could too much wine pass between my lips
kingfishers nest below the waterway pavilions
and the unicorns have fallen by the garden tomb
to ponder such things is to turn to pleasure
what use is mere fame if it weighs a person down

195

曲江（二） 杜甫

朝回日日典春衣 每日江頭盡醉歸
酒債尋常行處有 人生七十古來稀
穿花蛺蝶深深見 點水蜻蜓款款飛
傳語風光共流轉 暫時相賞莫相違

In ancient times the Chinese made new clothes that they reserved for the end of spring. Nowadays they do the same, but they put them on as soon as the new year begins. At court this meant multiple sets of garments and various kinds of regalia. Tu Fu is so poor he pawns each set as soon as he's used it and buys wine to ensure his obliviousness to the sad state of affairs in the country and at court. Even his reappointment to the post of censor is no solace but, rather, a burden. Several months after he wrote this he was demoted and transferred to Huachou. But instead of taking up his new post a hundred or so kilometers east of Ch'ang-an, he resigned, left for Chengtu, and never returned to the capital, though he never stopped hoping to be recalled.

While Drinking at the Chuchiang Waterway—II

TU FU

Every day after court I pawn my spring clothes
every day from the waterway I come home drunk
wherever I go I owe money for wine
but living until seventy has always been rare
butterflies float half-seen among the flowers
dragonflies flit here and there across the water
I urge you to flow with the wind and light
enjoy your time together and don't fight

196

黃鶴樓　崔顥

昔人已乘黃鶴去　此地空餘黃鶴樓
黃鶴一去不復返　白雲千載空悠悠
晴川歷歷漢陽樹　芳草萋萋鸚鵡洲
日暮鄉關何處是　煙波江上使人愁

Ts'ui Hao (704–754) was from Kaifeng and moved to Ch'ang-an as a young man to take the civil service exam. Although he soon became a member of the salon of the Prince of Ch'i and a close friend of Wang Wei, his unconventional behavior resulted in a series of rustications, first to the frontier, then to various posts along the Yangtze. Here, he stands on the river's south shore, across from Hanyang, on a tower that commemorated the Taoist immortal Fei Wen-wei, who flew off from here on the back of a yellow crane, leaving the clouds behind. The locust and gingko trees on Hanyang's Phoenix Hill were so large their reflections reached the middle of the Yangtze. Parrot Isle, a sandbar in midstream, was a popular place to hold parties, until it disappeared in a flood. Li Pai liked this poem so much he quoted its ending in his own "Climbing Chinling's Phoenix Terrace." The mist reminds the poet of his loss of direction and of his separation from loved ones.

Yellow Crane Tower

TS'UI HAO

> A man rode off on a crane long ago
> Yellow Crane Tower is all that remains
> once the crane left it never returned
> for a thousand years clouds have wandered in vain
> the trees of Hanyang shine in midstream
> the sweet plants of spring overrun Parrot Isle
> at sunset I wonder which way is home
> mist on the river only means sorrow

197

自故蝴水
是園蝶流
不書夢花
歸動中謝
歸經家兩
便年萬無
得絕里情

春夕旅懷　崔塗

五華杜送
湖髮鵑盡
煙春枝東
景催上風
有兩月過
誰鬢三楚
爭生更城

Ts'ui T'u (fl. 900) was born along the Fuchiang River south of Hangchou but spent most of his life far from home. He witnessed the end of the T'ang dynasty and the rise of a series of independent states along the Yangtze, whose middle reaches were once controlled by the state of Ch'u, and where he now finds himself. In *Chuangtzu*: 2 a man wakes up from a butterfly dream to wonder if he isn't a butterfly dreaming he's a man. Here, the poet hears the cuckoo's cry, *pu-ju kuei-ch'u* ("better go home"), in the middle of the night. But why go home to a state where men compete over the meaningless mists of Lake Wuhu (aka Taihu) west of Suchou?

A Traveler's Thoughts on a Spring Evening

TS'UI T'U

Flowing water and falling petals have no pity
I see the East Wind off past the walls of Ch'u
a butterfly dreams ten thousand miles from home
a cuckoo perches beneath the midnight moon
no letters from home for more than a year
the gray at my temples all due to spring
I could go home if I wanted but don't
why fight over the mists of Wuhu

198

答李儋　　韋應物

去年花裏逢君別　今日花開又一年
世事茫茫難自料　春愁黯黯獨成眠
身多疾病思田里　邑有流亡愧俸錢
聞道欲來相問訊　西樓望月幾回圓

Wei Ying-wu (737–792) was from Ch'ang-an and wrote this in 785 when he was serving as magistrate of Suchou. He had been rusticated to the South in 781, and this was the last of a series of posts he held along the lower reaches of the Yangtze. Some commentators say this poem was written in 784 at his previous post in Chuchou, which also had a West Tower—but not one that faced the road from the capital to the northwest, as did Suchou's. The refugees were most likely the result of the wars that took place (781–786) between the T'ang court and the independent governors farther north along the Yellow River. But severe floods remain common in this region. Li Tan was a friend of the poet who was serving as a palace historian and with whom Wei exchanged poems.

In Reply to Li Tan

WEI YING-WU

We parted last year among flowers
this year they're blooming again
the haze of the world is hard to penetrate
troubled by the cares of spring I fall asleep alone
my body is ill my thoughts are in the fields
I'm ashamed of my salary with refugees in town
I heard you were planning to come for a visit
how many moons have I watched from West Tower

江村　杜甫

清江一曲抱村流
長夏江村事事幽
自去自來梁上燕
相親相近水中鷗
老妻畫紙為棋局
稚子敲針作釣鉤
但有故人供祿米
微軀此外復何求

After quitting his post in Huachou in 758, Tu Fu (712–770) stayed for a while in Tienshui then moved to Szechuan province in 759. With the help of a relative he managed to buy a small piece of land and build a cottage outside Chengtu's West Gate on the banks of the Huanhua River, a minor tributary of the nearby Min. He wrote this poem in 760 during his first summer there. His cottage, or at least a reconstructed version, is still on the same spot, and authorities have even begun excavating Tu Fu's old trash heap. Another variant of the seventh line reads: "all I need is medicine for my countless ills." Officials were paid in units of grain they could use as food or convert into currency.

River Village

TU FU

A clear river winds around the village
all summer long village life is peaceful
swallows in the rafters come and go at will
seagulls on the water visit friends and kin
my wife draws a chessboard on a piece of paper
my children make fishhooks out of sewing needles
thankfully an old friend shares his office rice
what else does this poor body need

夏日　張丰

長夏江村風日清
蝶衣曬粉花枝舞
落落疏簾邀月影
久斑兩鬢如霜雪

篁牙燕雀已生成
蛛網添絲屋角晴
嘈嘈虛枕納溪聲
直欲樵漁過此生

Chang Feng (1052–1112) was from Chingchiang in Kiangsu province and served in the Sung capital of Kaifeng, where he rose to the rank of vice-minister in charge of ritual observances. He was one of the four most famous members of Su Shih's literary coterie and was known for the realism of his poetry as well as for his honesty and love of simplicity. Not surprisingly, many of his surviving poems are about life in the country-side. This was one in a series of three he wrote soon after his retirement.

Summer Day

CHANG FENG

Late summer on the river the sun and wind are mild
the little birds below the eaves are grown
sun-drenched butterflies dance among the flowers
newly spun spiderwebs brighten every room
threadbare curtains invite the moon's reflection
a pillow made of clay echoes with the current
my long-graying temples recall the frost and snow
let me pass this life chopping wood and fishing

201

積雨輞川莊作　王維

積雨空林煙火遲　蒸藜炊黍餉東菑
漠漠水田飛白鷺　陰陰夏木囀黃鸝
山中習靜觀朝槿　松下清齋折露葵
野老與人爭席罷　海鷗何事更相疑

The retreat Wang Wei (701–761) bought on the Wang River was sixty kilometers southeast of Ch'ang-an and once belonged to the poet Sung Chih-wen. Although Wang rose to the post of deputy prime minister, he was a lifelong Buddhist and a vegetarian, and toward the end of his life he spent more time meditating at his retreat and hiking around the mountains than working in the capital. Hibiscus flowers only last a day, or two at most, and mallow leaves are best picked after the dew dries. Hence, Wang Wei is too hungry to wait. In *Chuangtzu*: 27 the arrogant Yang-tzu Yu returns to his inn after receiving instruction from Lao-tzu. But where he was once waited on hand and foot, he now has to fight for a place for his mat. "Seats" here also refer to positions of authority, concerning which the poet no longer has any interest. In *Liehtzu*: 2.11 the author recounts how seagulls flock around a man, until he conceives of a plan to catch them.

Written at My Wang River Retreat after a Steady Rain

WANG WEI

Steady rain deserted woods and finally kitchen smoke
steamed greens and millet for those in the eastside fields
snowy egrets fly above a sea of flooded fields
golden orioles sing in the shadows of summer trees
sitting in the mountains I regard the day's hibiscus
and cut dewy mallow leaves for a meal below the pines
living in the country I've stopped fighting over seats
why then do the seagulls still suspect me

202

東湖新竹　　陸游

插棘編籬謹護持　養成寒碧映漣漪
清風掠地秋先到　赤日行天午不知
解籜時聞聲簌簌　放梢初見影離離
官閒我欲頻來此　枕簟仍教到處隨

Lu Yu (1125–1210) was an orphan who was raised by monks at a monastery in Tienmen in Hupei province. He was one of the most romantic figures of his day and was known for his support of efforts to recover North China from the Khitans, as well as for the travel diary he wrote about his journey to Szechuan and for his book on tea. But he was also the most prolific lyric poet of the Sung and left behind nearly 10,000 poems. He spent the last twenty years of his life in Chekiang province in Shaohsing and built a retreat at the city's East Lake, which was once a quarry and was known for its precipitous rock formations, shaded bays, and bamboo-lined shores. Some editions attribute this poem to Huang T'ing-chien.

New Bamboo at East Lake

LU YU

I planted thorns and built a fence to keep them safe
their growing emerald canes shimmer in the ripples
autumn arrives first where a breeze cools the earth
the summer sun overhead is far away at noon
they make a rustling sound as they discard their wrappers
and cast spindly shadows as they put forth new branches
I plan to visit often as soon as I stop working
and take my mat and pillow when I go

203

夏夜宿表兄話舊　竇叔向

夜合花開香滿庭　夜深微雨醉初醒
遠書珍重何曾達　舊事淒涼不可聽
去日兒童皆長大　昔年親友半凋零
明朝又是孤舟別　愁見河橋酒幔青

Tou Shu-hsiang (fl. 780) was from Fenghsiang west of Ch'ang-an and was a close friend of Ch'ang Kun. When Ch'ang became prime minister, Tou was appointed censor. But when Ch'ang was ousted in 779, Tou was banished to Lishui, southeast of Nanching, where he wrote this poem. When officials were sent to such distant posts, family members usually remained behind. Despite his long absences, Tou's five children all became known for their poetry. The flowers here are identified by some as *Magnolia pumila* and by others as *Pergularis ordoratissia*. The blue flags are those of wine-shops on the Kan River, a tributary of the Chinhuai that flows northwest into the Yangtze at Nanching.

Spending a Summer Night with My Cousin Talking about the Past

TOU SHU-HSIANG

Magnolia perfume inundates the courtyard
the wine doesn't last through a late night drizzle
how can I reply to the distant words of loved ones
or bear to hear about the dismal past
our children all are grown
our friends are mostly gone
another boat leaves tomorrow
I hate those blue flags by the bridge

204

秋日偶成　程顥

閒來無事不從容　睡覺東窗日已紅
萬物靜觀皆自得　四時佳興與人同
道通天地有形外　思入風雲變態中
富貴不淫貧賤樂　男兒到此是豪雄

Ch'eng Hao (1032–1085) taught thousands of students at his home in Loyang and served briefly in the nearby capital of Kaifeng. But due to his opposition to the policies of Wang An-shih, he was banished to South China and died before he could return. Still, with his younger brother, Ch'eng Yi, he was among the leading lights of neo-Confucianism. This poem reflects his philosophy whereby all things are seen as part of the Tao and also as part of the mind. Thus, man shares the same nature as Heaven and Earth and all creation. The harmony of this nature is easily upset by desire and ignorance, but it can be restored through the cultivation of such virtues as kindness and equanimity. The last two lines paraphrase *Mencius*: 3b/2.3.

Occasional Poem on an Autumn Day

CH'ENG HAO

When I'm at peace I let everything go
I wake by the east window long after sunrise
viewed without passion everything is fine
seasonal glories hold true for man
the Tao fills the world the formed and the formless
our thoughts are in the ever-changing wind and clouds
not troubled by wealth content in poverty
the person who reaches this is truly noble

205

遊月陂　程顥

月陂堤上四徘徊　北有中天百尺臺
萬物已隨秋氣改　一樽聊為晚涼開
水心雲影閒相照　林下泉聲靜自來
世事無端何足計　但逢佳節約重陪

Crescent Pond was located inside the palace grounds in Kaifeng where Ch'eng was serving at the time. The tower he refers to was Iron Pagoda, which was part of Kaipao Temple northeast of the palace. The tower was originally built of wood c. 975. After a fire, it was rebuilt of bricks in 1049 and covered with glazed tiles that made it look as though it were made of iron. The rebuilt version, which Ch'eng sees in the distance and which still stands, is 56 meters high, whereas the original was 120 meters.

Visiting Crescent Pond

CH'ENG HAO

We circle the shore of Crescent Pond
to the north is a tower that touches the sky
the world has changed in the autumn air
we pour a cup for the evening chill
the image of a cloud pauses on the water
the sound of a stream lingers beneath the trees
our tasks are endless there's no need to count
let's meet again our next day off

206

秋興（一）　杜甫

玉露凋傷楓樹林　巫山巫峽氣蕭森
江間波浪兼天湧　塞上風雲接地陰
叢菊兩開他日淚　孤舟一繫故園心
寒衣處處催刀尺　白帝城高急暮砧

After leaving Chengtu in 765, Tu Fu (712–770) traveled down the Yangtze with his family and stopped in Fengchieh. He stayed there for two years as the guest of the prefect and during his second autumn wrote a series of eight poems, four of which appear here. The place where he lived was a few kilometers east of Fengchieh in the town of Paiti, overlooking the western entrance to the first of the Three Gorges. Wuhsia, or Sorceress Gorge, is the second of the three and was named for a mountain that served as a fair-weather beacon for river travelers. Paiti was once the capital of an independent state and also where Liu Pei died while trying to reunite China in the third century. Jade Dew is another name for the solar period known as White Dew that occurs in early September — when the leaves turn red and chrysanthemums bloom. Women used mallets of wood or stone to beat clothes while washing them or to toughen new material.

Autumn Inspiration — 1

TU FU

Jade dew wounds a forest of maples
Sorceress Mountain looks bleak in the gorge
waves in the river crash against the sky
clouds in the passes darken the earth
chrysanthemums once more have seen my tears about the past
my boat is still tied to thoughts of my garden
everywhere people are making winter clothes
in Paiti at dusk the mallets beat faster

207

秋興（二）　杜甫

千家山郭靜朝暉　日日江樓坐翠微
信宿漁人還泛泛　清秋燕子故飛飛
匡衡抗疏功名薄　劉向傳經心事違
同學少年多不賤　五陵裘馬自輕肥

Tu Fu describes his daily visit to a pavilion in Paiti that overlooked the Yangtze. Fishermen often spent several nights on the river before returning. But the two nights also refer to Tu Fu's two-year stay in Paiti. The swallows of summer are also staying longer than expected. Liu Hsiang (79–6 B.C.) and K'uang Heng took part in reforming religious observances of the Han court and its interpretation of the Confucian canon, often through the submission of memorials. Even though Tu Fu grew up near Loyang, he spent much of his youth and early career in the village of Shaoling in the southern suburbs of Ch'ang-an. Wuling was the location of five Han-dynasty imperial tombs northwest of Ch'ang-an, and its name was later used for the capital and its elite. The robes are light because they're made of silk.

Autumn Inspiration—II

TU FU

A hillside town of a thousand homes rests in morning light
every day from the river tower I look out on the landscape
fishermen are still drifting after two nights away
and swallows are still flying in the cool fall air
K'uang Heng was heard but my voice is faint
Liu Hsiang could teach but I am ignored
and yet few friends of my youth are poor
in Wuling their robes are light and their horses well-fed

208

秋興（三）　杜甫

蓬萊宮闕對南山　承露金莖霄漢間
西望瑤池降王母　東來紫氣滿函關
雲移雉尾開宮扇　日繞龍鱗識聖顏
一臥滄江驚歲晚　幾回青瑣點朝班

Tu Fu imagines himself back at court. Penglai Hall was located to the rear of Taming Palace in Ch'ang-an. The name came from a mythical island off the Shantung coast where immortals lived. The Chungnan Mountains were south of Ch'ang-an. As they seemed impervious to change, they were often used as a metaphor for immortality. The bronze pillars were erected by Emperor Wu of the Han dynasty, for collecting pure dew to use in elixirs. The Queen Mother of the West (Hsi-wang-mu) dispensed an elixir that ensured long life and lived at Jade Lake somewhere in Central Asia. Hanku Pass in westernmost Honan province was reportedly where Lao-tzu wrote the *Taoteching* before he disappeared into the mountains. Lao-tzu was especially honored during the T'ang, as his last name, Li, was the imperial family's surname. Pheasant tails were used for fans. The dark waters refer to those of Ch'u Yuan's "The Fisherman," which recalls the dilemma of the exiled poet who would still save his lord from disaster. And the last line concerns the poet's dreams.

Autumn Inspiration—III

TU FU

Penglai Hall looks south toward the mountains
its pillars of bronze collect dew from the stars
to the west the Queen Mother appears at Jade Lake
to the east purple mist fills Hanku Pass
a cloud of pheasant fans parts before the throne
sunlit dragon scales reflect our sage's face
living by dark waters I fear the year is late
I often return to court below the painted gates

209

秋興（四）　杜甫

昆明池水漢時功　武帝旌旗在眼中
織女機絲虛夜月　石鯨鱗甲動秋風
波飄菰米沉雲黑　露冷蓮房墜粉紅
關塞極天惟鳥道　江湖滿地一漁翁

Emperor Wu of the Han dynasty (r. 140–87 B.C.) constructed an artificial lake southwest of Ch'ang-an to conduct naval maneuvers and named it after the kingdom in Southwest China he planned to attack. On the east and west shores were statues that resembled the Weaving Maid and Herdboy — the two lovers forever separated by the Milky Way — and in the middle was a stone whale covered with jade scales. During the T'ang the lake was better known for its Manchurian wild rice, *Zizania latifolia*, and lotuses, both of which were harvested in the fall. Here, though, they have been neglected, as the country is in chaos. Tu Fu feels cut off from the capital in the North and adrift in the watery Yangtze watershed synonymous with recluses, bandits, and exiled officials.

Autumn Inspiration—IV

TU FU

Kunming Lake was the jewel of the Han
Emperor Wu's banners appear before my eyes
the Weaving Maid weaving in vain below the moon
the stone whale shimmering in the autumn wind
scudding black clouds of windswept wild rice
drifting pink powder from dry lotus pods
but sky-high passes are only for birds
rivers and marshes are a fisherman's world

210

月夜舟中　戴復古

満船明月浸虚空　綠水無痕夜氣沖
詩思浮沈檣影裏　夢魂搖曳拽櫓聲中
星辰冷落碧潭水　鴻雁悲鳴紅蓼風
數點漁燈依古岸　斷橋垂露滴梧桐

Tai Fu-ku (1167–1248) was from Huangyen in Chekiang province. He spent many years roaming the rivers and lakes of the lower reaches of the Yangtze and was the most celebrated member of the Rivers and Lakes school of poetry. Especially famous are his poems criticizing the life of ease of the Sung court and its refusal, or inability, to retake North China from the barbarians. Tai wrote this poem at Hangchou's West Lake. Chinese boats often use a single scull at the stern for propulsion, rather than a pair of oars. Water pepper is the common name for *Polygonum hydropiper*, a variety of knotweed or smartweed. Broken Arch Bridge connected the Southern Sung capital to the small island of Kushan, which was once the home of the reclusive poet Lin Pu (967–1028).

Aboard a Boat on a Moonlit Night

TAI FU-KU

Moonlight fills the boat and floods an empty sky
night air pours across the green and glassy water
ideas for a poem sway in the shadows of the mast
my dream spirit rows to the sound of the scull
stars are scattered on the jade-colored lake
wild geese cry out in the water-pepper wind
a few fishing lanterns mark the ancient shore
dew drips from paulownias on Broken Arch Bridge

211

長安秋望　趙嘏

雲物凄涼拂曙流　漢家宮闕動高秋
殘星幾點雁橫塞　長笛一聲人倚樓
紫艷半開籬菊靜　紅衣落盡渚蓮愁
鱸魚正美不歸去　空戴南冠學楚囚

Chao Ku (815–856) was from Huai-an in Kiangsu province, which was once part of the ancient state of Ch'u. Although he wrote this while serving as commandant of Weinan just east of Ch'ang-an, his sentiments must have changed, as this was where he later retired. During the Western Chin dynasty (265–316) Chang Han was serving one autumn in Loyang, when he thought about sea perch stew on the Grand Canal. He became so homesick he quit his post and went home. Chao recalls Chang's example but is unable to emulate it and likens himself, instead, to Chung Yi. Chung was the prime minister of Ch'u, captured during a war with the state of Cheng and given to the state of Chin. When the Duke of Chin saw him, the duke asked, "Who is this in chains wearing a strange hat?" An attendant answered, "A prisoner from Ch'u" (*Tsochuan*: King Ch'eng, Ninth Year).

Autumn Longing in Ch'ang-an

CHAO KU

Desolate cloud shapes brush past the dawn
the full force of autumn descends on the palace
a few fading stars and migrating geese
leaning from a tower I hear a flute
chrysanthemums are silently starting to turn purple
without their pink robes lotuses look sad
sea perch are in season but I can't go home
a prisoner from Ch'u I wear a strange hat

212

新秋　杜甫

火雲猶未斂奇峰　欹枕初驚一葉風
幾處園林蕭瑟裏　誰家砧杵寂寥中
蟬聲斷續悲殘月　螢燄高低照暮空
賦就金門期再獻　夜深搔首歎飛蓬

Tu Fu (712–770) wrote this poem in 761 in Chengtu. Some editions, however, attribute it to Sun Chin (960–1017). As autumn brings relief from summer heat, Tu Fu is more concerned that the time has nearly passed for an appointment equal to his aspirations. Hence, he considers submitting a poem to the throne, as he had done previously without success—and as the poet Ssu-ma Hsiang-ju (179–117 B.C.) once did during the Han dynasty at Chinma (Bronze Horse) Gate outside the Secretariat. The Chinese pounded their clothes on flat rocks when washing them, but they also pounded new material in autumn to toughen the fabric for winter. The last line quotes a poem in the *Book of Odes* that expresses disappointment in growing old without achieving one's ambition.

Early Autumn

TU FU

Before the fiery clouds have quenched their fearsome peaks
resting on a pillow I'm surprised by a breeze
somewhere garden trees are sighing
and someone pounds a solitary mallet
throbbing cicadas mourn the setting moon
zigzagging fireflies light the evening sky
I planned to take a poem to Chinma Gate again
but late at night I scratch my head and sigh at my thin hair

213

中秋　李朴

皓魄當空寶鏡升
平分秋色一輪滿
狡兔空從弦外落
靈槎擬約同攜手

雲間仙籟寂無聲
長伴雲衢千里明
妖蟆休向眼前生
更待銀河徹底清

Li P'u (1063–1127) was from Kanchou in Kiangsi province and was known as an honest, forthright official. Here, he describes the eighth full moon, the celebration of which is second only to the lunar New Year in the Chinese calendar. The autumn equinox also takes place around this lunar holiday. The hare that lives on the moon produces the elixir of immortality. When the moon is full the hare is upside down and looks as if it is falling off. The three-legged toad, which consumes the hare's elixir, is visible earlier in the month but hard is to make out when the moon is full. It's said that the sea and sky were once joined and that immortals went back and forth on a magic raft. The Silver River is the Milky Way, which is only navigable when the sky is clear.

Mid-Autumn

LI P'U

A bright spirit in the sky a jeweled mirror rising
silences the music of immortals in the clouds
a perfect wheel at the height of autumn
shines for a thousand miles on a never-ending path
the clever hare falls off its rim
the ugly toad stays out of sight
let's go together on a magic raft
the next time the Silver River is clear

214

明年此會知誰健　醉把茱萸仔細看
藍水遠從千澗落　玉山高並兩峰寒
羞將短髮還吹帽　笑倩旁人為正冠
老去悲秋強自寬　興來今日盡君歡

九日藍田崔氏庄　杜甫

Tu Fu (712–770) wrote this poem in 758 while attending a banquet in Lantien, southeast of Ch'ang-an at the foot of the Chungnan Mountains. Lantien was named for a nearby mountain known for its jade and was also called Yushan, or Jade Mountain. The banquet was held at a friend's villa to celebrate the ninth day of the ninth month, the ultimate *yang* holiday. According to ancient custom, men consumed a decoction of prickly ash (*Zanthoxylum ailanthoides*) and drank chrysanthemum-infused wine on this day to expel evil influences and to lengthen their lives. A hat was a gentleman's badge of honor, and to be without one was considered a breach of etiquette. Once, when Chia Meng was at a banquet his hat blew off. Instead of apologizing or being embarrassed he acted as if nothing had happened. Tu Fu shows similar nonchalance by doing the opposite.

At Mister Ts'ui's Villa in Lantien on the Ninth

TU FU

An old man mourning fall I try to console myself
happy to have shared this day with friends
thinking my hair too short or my headgear insecure
I laughed and asked someone to fix my hat
blue water falls from a thousand distant streams
Jade Mountain is high and its two peaks are cold
this time next year who will still be healthy
let's find some prickly ash after we get drunk

215

秋思　陸游

利欲驅人萬火牛
江湖浪跡一沙鷗
日長似歲閒方覺
事大如天醉亦休
砧杵敲殘深巷月
梧桐搖落故園秋
欲舒老眼無高處
安得元龍百尺樓

Lu Yu (1125–1210) was one of the most beloved poets of the Sung dynasty but was too much of an idealist to ever achieve high office. Here, he turns to the countryside for solace. In 279 B.C. the state of Ch'i outfitted a herd of oxen with knives on their horns and oil-soaked rushes on their tails, then set fire to the rushes and drove the oxen into the army of the state of Yen and routed it. The Chinese used wooden or stone mallets to launder clothes, but they also used them for toughening material for winter. Paulownia leaves are bigger than dinner plates. Once, when Hsu Fan was a guest of Ch'en Yuan-lung, Yuan-lung made him sleep on the lower bunk. When Hsu later complained to Liu Pei, Liu reprimanded him, saying, "It's a small-minded person who wants to sleep in a hundred-foot tower." Here, Lu turns this around to his own amusement.

Autumn Thoughts

LU YU

Like oxen on fire we're driven by desire
or we drift like seagulls among rivers and lakes
days can last years when a person finds peace
great concerns vanish for those who stay drunk
mallet sounds fade below a country-lane moon
paulownia leaves blanket my garden in fall
I need somewhere high to let my eyes roam
where can I find Yuan-lung's old tower

216

南鄰　杜甫

錦里先生烏角巾
園收芋栗未全貧
慣看賓客兒童喜
得食階除鳥雀馴
秋水纔深四五尺
野航恰受兩三人
白沙翠竹江村暮
相送柴門月色新

Tu Fu (712–770) wrote this poem in 762 when he was living in his cottage on the Huanhua River just outside the West Gate of Chengtu, the capital of Szechuan province. A kilometer or two to the south, his reclusive friend Chu Hsi-chen lived on the Chin River. Wearing some sort of hat or head covering was so universal among men in ancient China that even recluses wore something, usually a simple bandanna that they knotted on either side of the head and that looked like a pair of horns. The chestnuts here are water chestnuts. Tu Fu likens his friend to one of the Four Worthies of the Chungnan Mountains who was known as Mister Chiao Village.

For Hermit Chu, My Neighbor to the South

TU FU

Mister Chin Village with his blackhorned bandanna
grows taro and chestnuts and can't be called poor
his children are glad to see a guest arrive
and birds aren't afraid to eat food on his steps
the river in autumn isn't five feet deep
and the ferry holds maybe three people
in the sand and bamboo and the river-village dusk
he sees me to his gate when the moon is new

誰家吹笛畫樓中　　斷續聲隨斷續風
響過行雲橫碧落　　清和冷月到簾櫳
興來三弄有桓子　　賦就一篇懷馬融
曲罷不知人在否　　餘音嘹喨尚飄空

聞笛　趙嘏

Chao Ku (815–856) was born in Huai-an in Kiangsu province. After passing the civil service exam in 842, he served in a number of posts and finally as commandant of Weinan just east of Ch'ang-an, where he eventually retired. Huan Yi (d. 392) was known for his military prowess and his adherence to decorum. He was also the most famous flautist of his time. Once, while traveling down a river Wang Hui-chih was informed of his presence in a nearby boat and sent a messenger to request an example of his skill. Huan replied by playing three tunes but made no attempt to meet the son of the famous calligrapher Wang Hsi-chih. Ma Jung (79–166) remains famous today for his commentaries on the Confucian classics, but he also wrote odes, one of them on the flute.

Hearing a Flute

CHAO KU

Whose flute is that in the painted tower
blowing and pausing in harmony with the wind
its sound stops the clouds traveling across the sky
its notes reach my curtain with the winter moon
inspired like the tunes of Huan Yi
reminiscent of Ma Jung's old ode
but where is the person when the song is done
and the notes continue to float in the air

冬景　劉克莊

晴窗早覺愛朝曦　竹外秋聲漸作威
命僕安排新暖閣　呼童熨貼舊寒衣
葉浮嫩綠酒初熟　橙切香黃蟹正肥
蓉菊滿園皆可美　賞心從此莫相違

Liu K'o-chuang (1187–1269) was from Putien in Fukien province and was a leading literary figure of the late Sung dynasty. He was also the compiler of the original edition of *Poems of the Masters*. Hence, this poem must have been added sometime later. The sound of fall is that of the north wind. The "leaves" in the fifth line refers to tea leaves. The lower reaches of the Yangtze remain famous for freshwater crabs, which reach their peak of maturity in the ninth and tenth lunar months. Both their meat and their roe are still sought-after delicacies in Shanghai and other Delta cities this time of year. The rose mallow, or *Hibiscus mutabilis*, produces large rose-colored blooms in the eighth and ninth lunar months in China.

Winter Scene

LIU K'O-CHUANG

I love to wake to morning light beneath a frosted window
the sound of fall growing louder in the bamboo grove outside
I tell a serving maid to heat my new pavilion
and call a young attendant to iron last winter's clothes
the leaves are green and tender the wine is freshly made
the oranges sweet and golden the crabs are truly fat
and mallows and chrysanthemums lovely in the garden
may I never part from such delights again

小至　杜甫

天時人事日相催
冬至陽生春又來
刺繡五紋添弱線
吹葭六管動飛灰
岸容待臘將舒柳
山意衝寒欲放梅
雲物不殊鄉國異
教兒且覆掌中杯

Commenting on the hexagram *Fu* (The Return), the *Yiching*: 24 says, "When a single *yang* line appears below, this is the time of the winter solstice." Many customs developed in China in association with this solar date when days finally begin to grow longer again. On the solstice, women began embroideries to be completed by New Year, and men stuffed reed ashes into flutes and blew. The ashes were supposed to float upward if Heaven's and man's seasons were in harmony. Prior to the solstice they floated downward. The color and shape of clouds were also noted as forecasting prospects for the coming year. Tu Fu wrote this poem in 766 while staying in Fengchieh in the Yangtze Gorges. It was still unsafe to return to his home, as the An Lu-shan Rebellion had left North China at the mercy of local warlords as well as the Turks. Hence, Tu Fu has no enthusiasm for wine.

Winter Solstice Eve

TU FU

Heaven's times and man's affairs hurry us along
on winter solstice *yang* appears and spring returns
to silk embroideries a thread is added
out of long flutes reed ashes fly
the shores wait for New Year to set willows free
the hills battle cold to liberate plum trees
the shapes of clouds are the same as back home
I tell my son to finish my wine

山園小梅　林逋

眾芳搖落獨暄妍　占斷風情向小園
疏影橫斜水清淺　暗香浮動月黃昏
霜禽欲下先偷眼　粉蝶如知合斷魂
幸有微吟可相狎　不須檀板共金樽

Lin Pu (967–1028) spent most of his life near Hangchou and steadfastly refused to become an official, preferring to live as a recluse just outside the city's West Gate. During one stretch he didn't enter the city for twenty years. He also never married and doted instead on his pet cranes and plum trees. In the fifth and sixth lines, migrating birds confuse the shimmering white petals with snow, and if butterflies could only survive the cold, they would surely mistake the plum's blossoms for white-winged colleagues from a higher realm. Poets often tapped on a sounding board to keep time while singing poetry.

How Plum Flowers Embarrass a Garden

LIN PU

When everything has faded they alone shine forth
encroaching on the charms of smaller gardens
their scattered shadows fall lightly on clear water
their subtle scent pervades the moonlit dusk
snowbirds look again before they land
butterflies would faint if they but knew
thankfully I can flirt in whispered verse
I don't need a sounding board or winecup

左遷至藍關示姪孫湘　韓愈

一封朝奏九重天　夕貶朝陽路八千
本為聖朝除弊政　敢將衰朽惜殘年
雲橫秦嶺家何在　雪擁藍關馬不前
知汝遠來應有意　好收吾骨瘴江邊

Han Yu (768–824) was one of the most famous literati of the T'ang and an ardent Confucian. When Emperor Hsien-tsung (r. 805–820) welcomed the Buddha's finger-bone to the palace in 819, the ceremonies were too much for Han, and he submitted a memorial criticizing such worship, suggesting it would shorten the emperor's life span. For his temerity Han was banished to the southeast coast, from which many officials never returned. Here, he finds himself southeast of the capital, stuck at Lankuan Pass in the Chinling/Chungnan Mountains. While he was waiting for the snow to melt, his nephew, Han Hsiang, heard of his plight and paid him a visit. Han Hsiang later took up residence in a cave not far to the west of Lankuan Pass and was eventually ranked among Taoism's Eight Immortals.

For My Nephew, Hsiang, on My Demotion and Arrival at Lankuan Pass

HAN YU

I submitted a memorial to the palace at dawn
by dusk I was bound for Chaoyang two thousand miles away
I hoped to rid the court of evil ways
but dared in my senility to begrudge a few more years
Chinling clouds now bar me from my home
Lankuan snows still block the path ahead
there must be a reason you've traveled this far
no doubt to collect my bones from some infested river

干戈

王中

干戈未定欲何之　一事無成兩鬢絲
蹤跡大綱王粲傳　情懷小樣杜陵詩
鶺鴒音斷人千里　烏鵲巢寒月一枝
安得中山千日酒　酩然直到太平時

Wang Chung (fl. thirteenth century) lived in North China when the Mongols began a series of invasions that brought the Sung dynasty to an end. Wang Ts'an (177–217) wrote odes that described the suffering of people during war, and many of Tu Fu's (712–770) best-known poems described a country in turmoil and his own separation from home. In the *Book of Odes* the wagtail represents the closeness of brothers who sing out when one of them is in trouble. The magpie is wary of traps and builds its nest at the tops of trees where several branches join. But here it is forced to make do with a single branch. Ts'ao Ts'ao's "Short Ballad" is also in the backgound: "The moon is bright and stars are few / a magpie flies south / circling a tree three times / on which limb can it rest?" According to Chang Hua's *Powuchih*, a Taoist immortal named Chung-shan brewed a wine that could keep a person drunk for three years.

Spears and Shields

WANG CHUNG

Where can I go when spears and shields are clashing
my one success has been to turn my temples white
my steps more or less have followed a Wang Ts'an ode
and my heart feels like a Tu Fu poem
a wagtail can't be heard a thousand miles away
a magpie spends the winter on a single moonlit branch
where can I get some of Chung-shan's Three Year Wine
and stay completely drunk until peaceful times begin

223

歸隱　陳摶

十年蹤跡走紅塵
回首青山入夢頻
紫綬縱榮爭及睡
朱門雖富不如貧
愁聞劍戟扶危主
悶聽笙歌聒醉人
攜取舊書歸舊隱
野花啼鳥一般春

Ch'en T'uan (871–989) was from Liuyi in Honan province, Lao-tzu's old hometown. Although he hoped to become an official during the Later T'ang dynasty (923–935), he was so disappointed by the chaos of the times that he returned to the hermitage he had built earlier at the foot of Huashan and lived there as a recluse for the rest of his long life. Ch'en cultivated Taoist meditation and often remained in a sleeplike trance for months. His *Wuchitu* (*Diagram of the Limitless*) was a major influence on early proponents of neo-Confucianism. Red dust refers to the world of the senses, purple cords were attached to the seals of high officials, and red paint was reserved for the households of the elite. The "spring" of the last line refers to the season.

Returning to My Retreat

CH'EN T'UAN

Through the red dust I tramped for ten years
green mountains though were often in my dreams
a purple cord brings fame but can't compare to sleep
crimson gates are grand but having less is better
how sad to hear swords guarding a feeble lord
how depressing the songs of noisy drunks
I'm taking my old books back to my retreat
to wildflowers and birdsongs and the same old spring

224

山中寡婦　杜荀鶴

夫因兵死守蓬茅　麻苧裙衫鬢髮焦
桑柘廢來猶納稅　田園荒盡尚徵苗
時挑野菜和根煮　旋砍生柴帶葉燒
任是深山更深處　也應無計避征徭

Tu Hsun-ho (846–907) was from Shihtai, just south of the Yangtze port of Kueichih and the sacred mountain of Chiuhuashan, in whose foothills he spent most of his life studying for the civil service exams. When he finally passed at the age of forty-five, he was appointed to the Hanlin Academy under the patronage of the former warlord Chu Wen (852–912), whose political machinations also brought the T'ang dynasty to an end. Tu's poetry, nearly all of which dates from before his success in the exams, is noteworthy for its focus on the distress of common people and the disorder of the times. It was common for the bereaved, after the death of a parent or spouse, to live in a thatched hut for up to three years and to wear rough hemp. Mulberry trees were used to feed silkworms. Taxes were imposed on land regardless of crop yields, and "seedling money" was often assessed by local officials and landlords when revenues fell short. Also, corvée — forced labor on government work projects — was calculated according to the number of males in a family.

A Mountain Widow

TU HSUN-HO

My husband died in battle my home is now a hut
my clothes are made of hemp my hair is like a broom
they keep collecting taxes on mulberry stumps
and still expect seedlings from overgrown fields
every day I forage for roots and plants to eat
or chop green wood and gather leaves to burn
even in the deepest depths of the mountains
there's nowhere to go to escape corvée

Postscript

The system of romanization used in this book to represent the sounds of modern Chinese is a modified version of the one that first appeared in R.H. Mathews's *Chinese-English Dictionary* (1931), which itself was based on the earlier publication of Thomas Wade's *Syllabary* (1867) and Herbert Giles's *Chinese-English Dictionary* (1912). All romanization systems have their shortcomings, but I have found the Wade-Giles the least bizarre. According to this system, aspirated consonants are unvoiced (*t'* as in "toy", *ch'* as in "church") and unaspirated consonants are voiced (*t* as in "dog" and *ch* like *j* in "jam") — reflecting the system's European origin. The only unfortunate romanization is the letter *j*, which is pronounced *r*, as in "row." (Compare this to the *x*, the *z*, and the *q* of the Pinyin system devised by the Cultural Revolution's masters of torture and to which most scholars now adhere for fear of being out of step.) Vowels are generally longer than in English, but the final *e* or *u* is given little or no emphasis. Thus, the *tzu* in *Lao-tzu* is pronounced the same as the final sound of the word "adze." In the interest of simplicity I have omitted the umlauts of the Wade-Giles system. And for the names of places and books I have usually omitted apostrophes and hyphens and run words together (e.g. Loyang, instead of Lo-yang, but Ch'ang-an, as it has become customary and avoids ambiguity of where to break the syllables).

As far as I know, this edition is the first in a Western language to include translations of all 224 poems in the *Chienchiashih* (*Poems of the Masters*). Admiral Ts'ai T'ing-kan (1861–1935) translated all the four-line poems and published the resulting collection in 1932 with the University of Chicago Press, under the title *Chinese Poems in English Rhyme*.

Dozens of Chinese commentaries to the *Chienchiashih* have been published over the years, especially over the past few decades. Although most are too superficial to deserve mention, I have found the following five useful:

Chang Che-yung: *Ch'ien-chia-shih p'ing-chu* (Shanghai: Huatung Normal University Press, 1982);

T'ang Lin and Yao Feng: *Ch'ien-chia-shih chu-hsi* (Lanchou: Kansu People's Press, 1982);

Yang Hung-ju: *Ch'ien-chia-shih p'ing-yi* (Beijing: Huawen Publishing Company, 1999);

Wang Ch'i-hsing: *Ch'ien-chia-shih hsin-chu* (Wuhan: Hupei People's Press, 1981);

Wen Chieh: *Hsiang-chieh ch'ien-chia-shih* (Hong Kong: Wenkuang Publishing Company, 1987).

Timeline

Hsia Dynasty	C. 2200 B.C.
Chou Dynasty	1122–255 B.C.
Warring States Period	733–221 B.C.
Ch'in Dynasty	221–207 B.C.
Han Dynasty	206–220
Three Kingdoms Period	221–265
Wu Dynasty	222–277
Six Dynasties Period	222–589
Western Chin Dynasty	265–316
Chin Dynasty	278–419
Liang Dynasty	502–557
Ch'en Dynasty	557–588
Sui Dynasty	589–618
T'ang Dynasty	618–906
An Lu-shan Rebellion	755–762
Greater Yen Dynasty	755–762
Tali Period	766–779
Five Dynasties Period	907–960
Later T'ang Dynasty	923–1643
Sung Dynasty	960–1278
Southern Sung Dynasty	1127–1279
Yuan Dynasty	1280–1368

About the Translator

Bill Porter assumes the pen name Red Pine for his translations. He was born in Los Angeles in 1943 and grew up in Northern Idaho. He served a tour of duty in the U.S. Army, graduated from the University of California, Santa Barbara, and attended graduate school at Columbia University. Uninspired by the prospect of an academic career, he dropped out of Columbia in 1972 and moved to a Buddhist monastery in Taiwan. Following four years with the monks and nuns, he struck out on his own, eventually working at English-language radio stations in Taiwan and Hong Kong, which afforded him the opportunity to travel extensively throughout China. He has visited the homesteads and graves of all the major poets in this collection, as well as the places where they wrote many of these poems. A Chinese translation of his book *Road to Heaven* has re-inspired Chinese interest in their own hermit tradition.

In recent years, Bill Porter has devoted himself to the translation of Buddhist texts. Currently, he is is working on the Heart and Lankavatara sutras.

Index of Authors

Index of Titles

The Chinese character for poetry is made up of two parts: "word" and "temple" (or, originally as Red Pine notes in his preface, "from the heart"). It also serves as pressmark for Copper Canyon Press.

Founded in 1972, Copper Canyon Press remains dedicated to publishing poetry exclusively, from Nobel laureates to new and emerging authors. The Press thrives with the generous patronage of readers, writers, booksellers, librarians, teachers, students, and funders — everyone who shares the conviction that poetry invigorates the language and sharpens our appreciation of the world.

THE ALLEN FOUNDATION *for* THE ARTS

Lannan

NATIONAL
ENDOWMENT
FOR THE ARTS

PUBLISHERS' CIRCLE
The Allen Foundation for The Arts
Lannan Foundation
National Endowment for the Arts

EDITORS' CIRCLE
The Breneman Jaech Foundation
Cynthia Hartwig and Tom Booster
Emily Warn and Daj Oberg
Washington State Arts Commission

For information and catalogs:

COPPER CANYON PRESS
Post Office Box 271
Port Townsend, Washington 98368
360/385-4925
www.coppercanyonpress.org

This book is set in Minion, designed for digital composition by Robert Slimbach in 1989. Minion is a contemporary typeface retaining elements of the pen-drawn letterforms developed during the Renaissance. Phaistos, by David Berlow, is used for the book and section titles. Chinese language set in Taipei. Map by Molly O'Halloran. Book design by Valerie Brewster, Scribe Typography. Printed on archival-quality Glatfelter Author's Text at McNaughton & Gunn, Inc.